JOURNEY

in PRAYER

7 Days of Praying with Jesus

JOHN SMED *with*

JUSTINE HWANG and **LEAH YIN**

MOODY PUBLISHERS
CHICAGO

Edited by Mackenzie Conway
Interior design: Leah Yin Studio and Erik M. Peterson
Cover design: Thinkpen Design
Cover illustrations: Leah Yin Studio
Cover icons copyright © 2019 by Elena Shchukina / Shutterstock (1315748924, 1268508646, 1276687279, 1093022738).
Cover illustration of hands copyright © 2019 by oxygen_8 / Shutterstock (1096902533).
Cover illustration of crown copyright © 2019 by maglyvi / Shutterstock (1144843826).
All rights reserved for all of the above photos.

Library of Congress Cataloging-in-Publication Data

Names: Smed, John, author.
Title: Journey in prayer : 7 days of praying with Jesus / by John Smed ;
    with Justine Huang and Leah Yin.
Description: Chicago : Moody Publishers, [2020] | Includes bibliographical
    references. | Summary: "An Evangelism Tool for a New Generation. Today's
    seekers are far more likely to be open to prayer than a traditional
    gospel presentation. This beautifully designed short book is
    unintimidating, inviting, and effective. It's a seven-day journey
    through the Lord's prayer. Each day explores a new petition in the
    Lord's prayer and helps show the reader the prayer's importance and
    impact. The author offers reflection questions, prayer prompts, and
    sample prayers to help readers begin and deepen their personal journeys
    in prayer. It's a perfect resource for anyone exploring the Christian
    faith or young Christians learning to prayer. Plus it works well
    one-on-one and in small groups"-- Provided by publisher.
Identifiers: LCCN 2019055262 (print) | LCCN 2019055263 (ebook) | ISBN
    9780802419880 (paperback) | ISBN 9780802498809 (ebook)
Subjects: LCSH: Lord's prayer--Devotional literature. | Lord's
    prayer--Commentaries. | Prayer--Christianity.
Classification: LCC BV230 .S534 2020 (print) | LCC BV230 (ebook) | DDC
    226.9/606--dc23
LC record available at https://lccn.loc.gov/2019055262
LC ebook record available at https://lccn.loc.gov/2019055263

Originally delivered by fleets of horse-drawn wagons, the affordable paperbacks from D. L. Moody's publishing house resourced the church and served everyday people. Now, after more than 125 years of publishing and ministry, Moody Publishers' mission remains the same—even if our delivery systems have changed a bit. For more information on other books (and resources) created from a biblical perspective, go to www.moodypublishers.com or write to:

Moody Publishers
820 N. LaSalle Boulevard
Chicago, IL 60610

1 3 5 7 9 10 8 6 4 2

Printed in the United States of America

Dedication

To Edith Schaeffer & Donald Drew
who set me on this road,
To Archie Parrish who kept me at it,
To Justine who helps cut new trails,
Especially to Caron,
who walks this path with me.

The Journey Begins:
An Introduction

"And we've got to get ourselves
back to the garden."
—Joni Mitchell

MY JOURNEY IN PRAYER BEGAN IN A
MONASTERY GARDEN. Recalling the events leading

up to this meeting with God, I have grim memories of the
distressing behaviors of my teen years—unchecked passions
and selfishness combined for a recipe of self-induced misery.

After graduating from high school in 1971, I took a few
months off to work and save money for my "big trip" to Europe.
I had been looking forward to this trip for years. One hot
summer day, I was working with an Italian journeyman named
Luigi to install counters and benches at a convent across from
Cemetery Hill in Calgary, Alberta.

During our coffee break, I walked up the hill and took a look
around. I saw a cultivated garden that was shaded, cool, and
pleasant. The bower was filled with a bewildering variety of
flowers resplendent in summer array and shrubs laden with
roses. A path wound through the garden and circled round to
where it began. Placed at intervals along the path were various

statues of the saints and a cross. They were set back from the path, leaving room for visitors to stop and contemplate.

As I approached and entered the winding path, I felt a perceptible difference. I experienced a calming. Any wind died down and the entire atmosphere was enveloped in peace. I took a few more steps and experienced a complex of curious and pleasant sensations. Imperceptibly, I had crossed a line. This garden was a little world within the world. I was reluctant to leave even after I had realized that my coffee break was over. When I returned back to work, thoughts of the garden stayed with me.

Leading up to this afternoon, I had been troubled in heart and mind for some time and had become numb by the events of the past. The hound of guilt had me cornered. For months a feeling of anxiety had been with me every waking moment—and in every nightmare. I took it wherever I went, and it formed a knot in my gut. I couldn't escape it. I wanted desperately to rid myself of it. If I tried to evade it, it tightened all the more. This knot felt physical. It sat in the middle of my chest—about the size of a racket ball—and was as hard as India rubber.

I did not know it at the time, but my inner torment had a hidden purpose. God used this anxiety and called me through the sorrow. He wanted me to listen carefully.

When the work was finished that day, I went back up the hill—me and my inner knot. I approached the entrance to the garden and walked down the path, taking my time. Every few steps I paused to look around, to smell the fragrances, to listen to the quiet. Like earlier in the day, I immediately experienced a surrounding calmness. I couldn't name it, but I could feel it. I found myself suspended in a calm and sacred awareness. There was peace in this place. There was presence.

I felt like I could stay in this place for a year—maybe forever.

Before I entered, my soul was a storm. But this place was tranquil. Before I entered, my heart was dying. But this garden was filled with life. Before I entered, my mind was in chaos. This garden grew with ordered freedom. As I walked, I noticed the intentional design of the trees, shrubs, and flowers—nothing was random or out of place. Statues of the saints blended in. Plants shaded the trail. Color and fragrances merged.

I was the only person in the garden—but I didn't feel alone. The garden felt "personed" with a solidity and safeness. I became aware that the world is not an empty place. God inhabits the creation He has made. If we have eyes to see, He is everywhere —entire, conscious, and present. I also became aware that I was being spoken to, yet all was silent. Nothing was audible; still the voice was clear and invited me to reply.

In response, I collapsed to my knees and prayed aloud: "God, I'm wrecked. Broken. Please heal me. I am all misery. There's a knot of unhappiness in my gut. I've tried everything—but I can't get rid of it. If You take this away from me, I will give my life to You. If You heal me, I will give my life to others who feel the same despair."

As I prayed these few words, the knot disappeared. I felt it untie and lift away—in a timeless moment. The emptiness, the guilt, and anxiety, all gone—entirely, at once, and forever. Released from some dark claw, my soul drew in a deep breath. I sat motionless and allowed this peace to penetrate me, rising up through my heart and entering my consciousness: ransomed, healed, restored, forgiven.

God met me in the garden that day and brought me home. Up till then it had been a one-way conversation—God speaking to me. Now it was a two-way dialogue. One brief prayer and my wandering life became a journey in prayer—it became an adventure.

The silence is all there is. It is the Alpha and the Omega. It is God's brooding over the face of the waters. You take a step in the right direction to pray to this silence.[1]

Over the following weeks and months, I kept praying, but something was missing. I soon grew tired of short prayers for myself and my small world. There were rivers of feelings and thoughts within just waiting to come out, but I did not have the words. I wanted to learn how to navigate life by prayer. It was pretty clear I needed a guide and road map for this journey.

A few months after my first prayer in the garden, I traveled to Europe. I ski-bummed and hitchhiked my way around and eventually happened to find myself at L'Abri Fellowship, a Christian community in the Swiss Alps. L'Abri means "shelter" in French. This happens to be a community devoted to daily prayer. (I have long since discovered that my "happenings" are God's plan.) L'Abri Fellowship is where I learned to converse with God and meditate on His goodness and power.

Not long after, I "happened upon" Jesus' prayer, which is commonly referred to as the "Lord's Prayer." In this prayer are seven requests. In this prayer is the secret to discovering the heart of God. To pray these seven requests is to journey deeper into life with God and deeper into life in the world.

I believe Jesus gives us this prayer to guide us in our own prayer journey. He supplies a road map in a world with no direction of its own and teaches us how to navigate life through prayer.

This book is a brief guide to each of the seven steps outlined in the Lord's Prayer found in Matthew 6:9–13. I invite you to join me in this *Journey in Prayer*. If you do, I pray that your life, like mine, will never be the same.

JOHN SMED

OUR
FATHER
IN HEAVEN,

HALLOWED be your name.
Your **KINGDOM COME,**
your **WILL BE DONE,**
on earth as it is in heaven.
Give us this day our **DAILY BREAD,**
and **FORGIVE US** our debts,
as we also have **FORGIVEN**
OUR DEBTORS.
And **LEAD US** not into temptation,
but **DELIVER US** from evil.

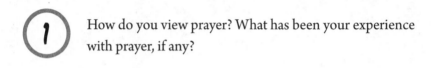

Prayerful Pondering

1 How do you view prayer? What has been your experience with prayer, if any?

2 What are the reasons you desire to pray?

3 What are you hoping for in your prayer journey as you delve into this book?

Ways to Use This Book

CREATIVE EXPLORATION

- Use the space provided throughout for your explorations: Highlight what resonates with you. Write your questions and key discoveries. Explore by doodling your prayers, meditations, and epiphanies.

- Prayer is conversation and relationship with God. Listen, receive, and record what God gives you. We hear from God through His thoughts written to us in His Word, the Bible, and the world around us. Like all conversations and relationships, prayer is organic, growing like a tree's branches and roots.

- We have left lots of free space throughout the book. Why? Jesus' prayer is simple, but it is also deep. It takes a lifetime to enjoy its riches. You may want to come back later to review a chapter or add to your prayer thoughts.

Prayer Practice

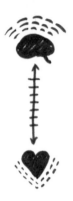

Prayer translates our thoughts into a deeper reality in our hearts and helps translate our head knowledge into heart experience of God.

Take a few moments after each chapter to practice prayer, using thoughts ignited by the questions and prompts to guide you.

Try writing out your prayers as a record of your communication and growing relationship with God. By the end of this book, you may be surprised by how you recognize God in new ways and see how He moves in your life as you pray.

My Personal Prayers

Borrow the prayers that express what is in your heart, or add your own.

TO FATHER GOD   **TODAY IS** MM / DD / YY

PRAY SPOT ☐ Work   ☐ Home   ☐ School   ☐ _____

MY PRAYER

DEAR GOD,

☐ I'M NOT SURE WHAT TO EXPECT WITH THIS PRAYER THING.

☐ I'M EXCITED TO SEE WHERE THIS JOURNEY IN PRAYER WILL LEAD.

☐

☐

☐

☐ HERE I AM WITH ALL MY UNCERTAINTIES AND HOPES: IF YOU'RE THERE, SPEAK TO ME IN A WAY THAT I CAN HEAR AND UNDERSTAND THAT IT'S YOU.

☐ I NEED   ☐ PEACE   ☐ STRENGTH   ☐ DIRECTION
         ☐   ☐   ☐
         ☐   ☐   ☐

. . . in Jesus' Name, Amen

Our Father in Heaven

*"This is the nature of the encounter,
not that I am stumbling towards the Abba Father,
but that Abba Father is running towards me."*
—Stephen Verney

PRAYER IS NOT ONE-WAY. IT IS TWO-WAY.

Think for a moment of the ways you picture prayer. Is it the penitent reciting the rosary? Is it monks spinning a prayer wheel? Is it the faithful bending low on prayer mats?

Though they may evoke powerful images, ritual incantations and relentless repetition are indications of "one-way" prayer. Prayer is not only about us getting through to God. Prayer is about God getting through to us so that we can discover His fatherly love for us. When we begin by praying "Our Father," we are asking that we might come to know God better.

Our prayers fail if they are just one-way. Theologian Martin Luther once said, "Few words and much meaning is Christian; many words and little meaning is pagan."[2] The prayer Jesus teaches us is two-way. In two-way communication, we look for a reply when we speak, and we come to realize that God is eager to know and enjoy us. As we grow in our comprehension of who God is, we begin to have comfort, freedom, and confidence in talking with Him. We gain assurance that we are heard by Him and that He will answer and give us what we need.

WE ARE ADOPTED—CHOSEN—BY OUR HEAVENLY FATHER

Several years ago, friends of mine named Stan and Lori Helm adopted their son Nicholas from Russia. By the time I met him, Nicholas was a beautiful little boy, full of life with curly auburn hair. It was hard to imagine the life he had left behind in the unsanitary orphanage, where he lived in ill health and covered in sores. He had seldom been held.

> As we grow in our comprehension of who God is, we begin to have comfort, freedom, and confidence in talking with Him.

I said to Stan, "Wow. Nicholas just won the adoption lottery with you and Lori."

Without a blink, Stan replied, "No, John. You're wrong. *We* won the lottery. No one in the world could be happier than we are to adopt him into our family."

His words struck me. It made me think about "sonship" with God. He is our adoptive Father. Could it be that God is just as thrilled as Stan and Lori?

THE NAME "FATHER" GETS GOD'S ATTENTION

My children are the only ones who use "Dad" when addressing me. In fact, it's the only name they use. If one of them calls me "mister," they probably won't get my attention. Unless I'm watching a hockey game, "Dad" gets through to me every time.

It is the same with God. We can try praying to a "higher power," we can meditate on the "ground of being," or we can study the "inner light." I doubt we will command God's attention with these generic phrases. We get God's full attention when we call Him by His favorite name—"Father."

In the same way, when Jesus prays to God, He calls Him "Father." Although there are seventy-two names for God in the Old Testament, and several more in the New Testament, every time Jesus addresses God, He calls Him "Father."

> "Father, I thank you that you have heard me." (John 11:41)
> "Father, if you are willing, remove this cup from me."
> (Luke 22:42)
> "Father, forgive them, for they know not what they do."
> (Luke 23:34)

HEAVENLY ADOPTION MADE POSSIBLE

How, then, do we gain the incredible privilege of calling God "Father"?

Simply this: When we trust in Jesus for forgiveness and eternal life, He confers upon us His own royal sonship status. By adoption, we become true sons and daughters of God. This means God views us the same as He views His only Son—along with all the benefits and access to Him that Jesus has. In his letter to the Galatian Christians, the apostle Paul explains this in dramatic terms:

> But when the fullness of time had come, God sent forth his Son, born of woman, born under the law, to redeem those who were under the law, so that we might receive adoption as sons. And because you are sons, God has sent the Spirit of his Son into our hearts, crying, "Abba! Father!" So you are no longer a slave, but a son, and if a son, then an heir through God. (Gal. 4:4–7)

Not only should this take our breath away, it is the key to all effective prayer. In prayer we now call God "Abba"—an affectionate term a Jewish child uses to say "daddy." We are able to leave behind our orphan aloneness and rest in the eternal "Daddyness" of our God.

WHAT THIS LOOKS LIKE WHEN IT COMES TO PRAYER

When you address God in this way, you are able to come to Him in freedom. You no longer have to plead your good works to earn your way in. Once you have trusted in Christ, you are God's child and nothing can ever take this from you. As the writer of the book of Hebrews said: "Let us then with confidence draw near to the throne of grace, that we may receive mercy and find grace to help in time of need" (Heb. 4:16).

When you talk to God, you no longer have to do penance and beat yourself up for your sins. You are forgiven the second you confess. God bears no grudge and remembers no sin. He allows you to leave behind the rituals and put on the full joy of being His child.

Once you have trusted in Christ, you are God's child and nothing can ever take this from you.

I think of our granddaughter Kaiya. When she comes into our home, she doesn't sit in a corner hiding, waiting for us to notice her—she runs up and seeks our attention. From her perspective, we have nothing more important to do and have been waiting for her all along. This is her privilege as our granddaughter. Kaiya can ask for anything she wants. We might say no because we love her and know what is best for her, but we would never ignore her, no matter what she asks.

When I pray "Our Father," I know I experience the results of having such a perfect Father. I learn to receive and rest in the presence of God—where I belong. I know I can confidently come to Him. He will never be too busy. My Father in heaven will never ignore me. I can humbly ask Him for anything I need. He is eager to listen. He is able to answer.

HE IS OUR FATHER "IN HEAVEN"

There are many weak and neglectful fathers in the world. But God, dwelling in the eternal reality of heaven, is the original perfect and changeless Father—"from whom every family in heaven and on earth is named" (Eph. 3:15). He will never abuse, neglect, or use you. His love for you will never corrupt or diminish.

"OUR FATHER" IS THE FIRST REQUEST OF THIS PRAYER

If it were up to us, we might want to jump right into prayers of confession—just to get rid of a bad conscience. We might start by crying out, "Help, Lord! I am drowning here. I need You now!" But Jesus teaches us to bond with God as Father, and if we start solidly with "Our Father," the rest of our prayer will be transformed.

As we pray each request of Jesus' prayer, we keep in mind that we are coming before a kind and generous Father. We ask boldly, because we know He is not offended. Teresa of Avila once said, "You pay God a compliment by asking great things of Him." Jesus said, "It is your Father's good pleasure to give you the kingdom" (Luke 12:32). Confident and effective prayer begins with "Our Father."

We start here. We can go no further until we know Him as Father. This precious truth should be carried into all our requests.

CONCLUSION

Remember Nicholas?

Stan and Lori went to Russia one last time to finish the adoption procedure. After finishing the paperwork, Stan stepped into the room and saw Nicholas in his orphan environment. He was covered in scabies—a bright red rash caused by small parasites. He had blisters on the bottom of his feet, the palms of his hands, and all over the inside of his mouth. He reeked. The orphanage did not have money for diapers, so he was often left in his own excrement.

With his voice breaking, Stan told me, "I just wanted to hold him. I wanted to comfort and heal him. But more than anything else, I wanted Nicholas to know just how much Lori and I love him."

What a beautiful picture of God's adoption of us. He sees us in the orphanage of the world. With a breaking heart, He notices the scabies of our discontent, the blisters of our unhappiness, and yes, the stench of the sin we have too long remained in. Rather than reject, despise, and judge us, He embraces us. He heals, cleans, and forgives us in His grace. He adopts us to be His sons and daughters. And He takes us home to live with Him forever. Now we call Him "Daddy."

Prayerful Pondering

DAY   1   2   3   4   5   6   7

1 How do you picture prayer—as a religious ritual/routine or as a two-way dialogue?

2 How do you feel about relating to God in a personal way?

Prayer Prompts

DAY (1) 2 3 4 5 6 7

WHEN WE PRAY "OUR FATHER IN HEAVEN":

- We thank God for His fatherhood. We thank Him for choosing us and adopting us into His family.

- We recognize there is nothing we can do to make God love us less or love us more than He already does.

My Personal Prayers

DAY (1) 2 3 4 5 6 7

Borrow the prayers that express what is in your heart, and add your own.

TO **FATHER GOD**   **TODAY IS**   MM / DD / YY

PRAY SPOT   ☐ Work   ☐ Home   ☐ School   ☐ _____

PATTERN   OUR FATHER IN HEAVEN
PRIORITY   KNOWING YOU IN A PERSONAL WAY
REQUEST   SHOW ME YOUR LOVE SO THAT I MAY TRUST AND KNOW YOU

MY LIFE

WHEN I THINK OF CALLING YOU FATHER:

☐ I'VE THOUGHT OF YOU AS IMPERSONAL OR DISTANT

☐ I'VE TREATED YOU AS A MAGIC GENIE, ONLY COMING TO
   YOU WITH WISHES

☐ ....

☐ ....

☐ ....

I AM FEELING ☐ EXCITED. ☐ AMAZED. ☐ UNSURE. ☐ AFRAID

☐   ☐

☐   ☐

THAT YOU WANT THIS PERSONAL RELATIONSHIP WITH ME.

My Personal Prayers

DAY   (1)   2   3   4   5   6   7

☐ SHOW ME WHO YOU ARE AND WHAT YOU'RE LIKE

☐ OPEN MY HEART TO EXPERIENCE YOUR LOVE IN A WAY
    THAT I CAN UNDERSTAND

☐

☐

MY GRATITUDE

FATHER, THANK YOU FOR:

MY RESPONSE

NEW REVELATIONS OR THOUGHTS, HEART CHANGES I FEEL
FROM YOU, OR STEPS I FEEL COMPELLED BY YOU TO TAKE:

. . . in Jesus' Name, Amen

Hallowed Be Your Name

*"Prayer will make a man cease from sin,
or sin will entice a man to cease from prayer."*
—John Bunyan

*"When we become too glib in prayer
we are most surely talking to ourselves."*
—A. W. Tozer

WHEN WE BEGIN OUR PRAYER WITH
"OUR FATHER," WE HAVE COMMUNION
WITH THE RELENTLESS AND PERFECT
LOVE OF THE FATHER. This love is revealed to us in
Jesus, delivered to us by Jesus, and is made ours forever in Jesus.
We now call God "Daddy"!

When we continue by praying "Hallowed be your name,"
we are asking that God's name be held in honor and reverence.

We seldom pay as much attention to God's holiness as we
do to His love. But the Old Testament highlights the holiness
of God. The prophet Isaiah calls God the "Holy One of Israel"
twenty-seven times! In a glorious and exalted vision of God,
Isaiah hears the seraphim, great angelic beings, continually
crying out: "Holy, holy, holy is the LORD of hosts; the whole
earth is full of his glory!" (Isa. 6:3).

In Hebrew thought, this threefold repetition is significant.
God is not holy in a comparative sense or in a superlative
sense. God is holy in a super-superlative sense. While angels
and men can participate in God's holiness, He is separate from
all creatures in His God-holiness. God's holiness is as rich and

complex as His infinite, eternal, and unchangeable being. It is revealed throughout the Bible.

SYMBOLS OF GOD'S HOLINESS

In the Old Testament there are three prominent symbols for God's holiness. These are precious jewels, blinding light, and intense fire. In one place, the prophet Ezekiel includes all three:

> And above the expanse over their heads there was the likeness of a throne, in appearance like sapphire; and seated above the likeness of a throne was a likeness with a human appearance. And upward from what had the appearance of his waist I saw as it were gleaming metal, like the appearance of fire enclosed all around. And downward from what had the appearance of his waist I saw as it were the appearance of fire, and there was brightness around him. Like the appearance of the bow that is in the cloud on the day of rain, so was the appearance of the brightness all around.
>
> Such was the appearance of the likeness of the glory of the LORD. And when I saw it, I fell on my face. (Ezek. 1:26–28)

First, precious jewels indicate the purity of God. The Bible says that heaven's streets are paved with pure gold "like transparent glass," its gates made of pure pearl, and its massive walls built of diamonds and jasper (Rev. 21:21). This is how God describes the purity and the holiness of His kingdom.

Second, the holy presence of God radiates a brilliant light—a light that radiates His very being. Anyone who sees the radiance of His glory fumbles around in "light blindness." The human eye cannot endure the supernova brightness of this light. Gazing at the splendor of God's holiness is more than any person can survive. God Himself says, "No one may see me and live" (Ex. 33:20 NIV).

The third symbol for God's holiness is a fierce fire that, like Moses and the burning bush, attracts and repels at the same time. In the New Testament, we are encouraged to draw near to God, but to do it "with reverence and awe, for our God is a consuming fire" (Heb. 12:28–29). His holiness is a burning passion for love, justice, righteousness, and truth. But we are warned that His fire is destructive toward anything unholy. It consumes any form of oppression, hatred, malice, envy, and greed.

When we put these three symbols together—precious jewels, brilliant light, and consuming fire—we are overcome by the beauty and power of God's holiness. To behold the radiant splendor of God is an experience that prompts us to fall down in awe and reverence. At the same time, to even get a glimpse of God's holiness is to yearn for more.

LONGING FOR HOLINESS

On one hand, God is separate from us because, in an absolute and qualitative sense, He alone is holy in a way we can never be. On the other hand, God calls us to participate in and reflect His holiness: "Be holy, because as I am holy" (1 Peter 1:16 NIV).

Our first parents, Adam and Eve, were created in innocence and holiness. When they disobeyed God, they fell from this perfect state—an entire world fell with them.

Imagine all humankind hurtling down a mountain road in a bus. The bus is piloted by Adam and Eve. Suddenly, the brakes fail and we slam through a concrete median and plunge down a cliff. Inside is a mangled mess. Everyone is crippled, torn, and scarred by this fall—some fare worse than others.

This is analogous to our spiritual nature. We are broken in the original fall of mankind. Crippled by sin, we are utterly unable to walk the path of holiness on our own.

However, no matter how broken and bruised, we are still irresistibly attracted to the glory and beauty of God's holiness. We hunger for our original fellowship with God. This is a dilemma great enough to fill a world of tragedies. We are like moths drawn to a flame. We are wary of approaching the fire because our wings are flammable. At the same time, we cannot survive or be happy without its light and heat.

Though we yearn to ascend to heaven and become one with God in His holiness, we are not made for the journey. We don't have the right stuff to withstand the supernova brightness or heat of His presence.

WE PRAY TO PARTAKE IN GOD'S HOLINESS

So how can we fulfill our longing to draw near to God's holiness without being consumed?

Isaiah asks the same question: "Who of us can dwell with everlasting burning?" His answer: "Those who walk righteously and speak what is right" (Isa. 33:14–15 NIV).

The solution to our need for holiness is Jesus. He alone has clean hands and a pure heart. He suffered an innocent death to remove our sin, as a substitute for any who will trust in Him. At the moment of true belief, a believer's sin is transferred to His account.

This transference of our guilt to Christ was foreshadowed in Old Testament times by the ritual of animal sacrifices. Whenever worshippers offered an animal as a sacrifice to God, they would lay their hands on it while it was living. By this act they were identifying with the animal and allowing the animal to pay the penalty for their sin. Laying hands on the living animal before it was killed signified the transfer of sin to the animal. After this, the animal was required to die to remove the sin of the one who offered it, dying in the place of the man or woman. (There are numerous examples of this in the book of Leviticus.) On the Day of Atonement, the high priest represented all the people of Israel at one time. He would lay his hands on the head of the goat offered to remove all the sins of the entire nation.

> **The solution to our need for holiness is Jesus. He alone has clean hands and a pure heart.**

Jesus takes away the sin of the one who believes in Him. We lay our sins on Jesus, and He takes them onto Himself and bears them away forever on the cross. More than this, Jesus also transfers to us His innocence. By faith in Christ, God accepts us as holy before Him. This two-way exchange—our sin for Jesus' righteousness—is the full story of how we are forgiven and saved from our sins. "For our sake [God] made him to be sin who knew no sin, so that in him we might become the righteousness of God" (2 Cor. 5:21). By placing our faith in Jesus, our sins are removed and we receive His perfect righteousness. Now we dare to approach God's holy presence—with boldness!

> Since then we have a great high priest who has passed through the heavens, Jesus, the Son of God. . . . Let us then with confidence draw near to the throne of grace, that we may receive mercy and find grace to help in time of need. (Heb. 4:14, 16)

Apart from Jesus, we are earthbound and cannot ascend to God. We do not have the wings necessary to take flight and reach these great heights. Forgiven of sin, covered with Jesus' innocence, we are given wings from heaven to fly ever upward. We not only ascend to God's holy presence. We live in His presence continually, as God has "seated us with him in the heavenly places in Christ Jesus" (Eph. 2:6).

WE GROW IN HOLINESS BY OBEYING THE TEN COMMANDMENTS

God has spelled out what holiness looks like and how a believer can grow in holiness by giving His people laws to live by. This is not just an Old Testament idea. Jesus said, "If you love me, you will keep my commandments" (John 14:15). God's holy requirements are comprehensively revealed in the Ten Commandments, which show us what our holy Father requires of us and what He forbids.

Commands one through four are about keeping God's name holy. First, we are to worship Him alone. Second, we are not to identify Him with nature or anything man-made. Third, we are not to represent or misuse His name in any way. Fourth, we are to set aside one day in seven for worship, rest, and good works.

Commands five through ten are about honoring God's image in the people He has made. Fifth, we are to honor our parents. Sixth to tenth, we are forbidden to kill, commit adultery, steal, falsely accuse, or envy our neighbour. In a positive way, we are actively to preserve and protect our neighbor's life, spouse, property, and reputation.

Because each of us is made in God's image, God's holy likeness is in every human being. Every man, woman, and child, no matter how broken and bruised by sin, still bears the mark of His image and must be loved and honored for God's sake. Our concern for the name of God results in love and concern for our fellow man.

JESUS CHRIST REVEALS GOD'S HOLINESS

Jesus reveals the full glory and holiness of God, in His perfect person and perfect nature. Notice how John the apostle describes Jesus' holy life in the same symbols and language used of God:

> We have seen his glory, the glory of the one and only Son, who came from the Father, full of grace and truth. . . . For the law was given through Moses; grace and truth came through Jesus Christ. No one has ever seen God, but the one and only Son, who is himself God and is in closest relationship with the Father, has made him known.
> (John 1:14, 17–18 NIV)

Therefore, it is Jesus who supremely reveals and defines holiness for the believer. Holiness is not just a matter of keeping commandments. Holiness involves following Jesus and becoming like Jesus. As we live in the presence and power of Jesus, we become, as the apostle Peter writes, "partakers of the divine nature" (2 Peter 1:4).

The gift of Christ's holiness is like a seed sown into the human heart. In time, through prayer and the Holy Spirit, the seed sprouts, grows, and bears leaves and fruit.

POWER FOR GOD'S HELP TO LIVE HOLY LIVES

We are no more able to be holy in our own strength than we are able to escape earth's gravity. In order to break through the force of gravity, a rocket needs to reach escape velocity of twenty-five thousand miles per hour. This requires rocket fuel. To overcome the immense gravity of our weakness and sin, we need more than natural power. In our fallen nature, we are too weak. We need supernatural power. This is why we ask continually to "be filled with the Spirit" (Eph. 5:18). When we pray "Hallowed be your name," we acknowledge God's power and ask for His power to fill us. When we do, we will be filled with the courage and strength needed for a life of holiness. This is what happened to the early church, and it will happen again today. Consider this remarkable example from the book of Acts:

> We are no more able to be holy in our own strength than we are able to escape earth's gravity.

> When they heard this, they raised their voices together in prayer to God. . . . After they prayed, the place where they were meeting was shaken. And they were all filled with the Holy Spirit and spoke the word of God boldly. All the believers were one in heart and mind. No one claimed that any of their possessions was their own, but they shared everything they had. With great power the apostles continued to testify to the resurrection of the Lord Jesus. And God's grace was so powerfully at work in them all that there were no needy persons among them. For from time to time those who owned land or houses sold them, brought the money from the sales and put it at the apostles' feet, and it was distributed to anyone who had need.
> (Acts 4:24, 31–35 NIV)

Joyous fellowship, sacrificial generosity, practicing God's holiness in practical and radical ways: This is what it means to follow Jesus. This is what holiness is all about.

WORSHIP GOD'S HOLINESS

When we think of worship, we might only think about a Sunday morning church service. However, there are two kinds of worship in the Bible. The first denotes a life of worship. In this sense we are to offer our words, thoughts, and deeds in a daily way to God: "I appeal to you therefore, brothers, by the mercies of God, to present your bodies as a living sacrifice, holy and acceptable to God, which is your spiritual worship. Do not be conformed to this world, but be transformed by the renewal of your mind" (Rom. 12:1–2).

The second kind of worship is praising, proclaiming, and singing the wonders of God's person and His actions. Like the angels, we are to sing: "Holy, holy, holy is the LORD of hosts" (Isa. 6:3).

This is where our prayer ultimately leads and finds its fulfillment—to joyous praise of God.

Prayerful Pondering

1 Our hearts were made for worship—we all worship something. What do your prayers, thoughts, words, and actions reveal about what or who you worship?

2 Would you consider yourself to be a righteous person? How do you see yourself in light of God's perfect holiness?

3 Where in the world around you do you wish for God's holiness and justice to break through? Where do you need courage to stand for righteousness and justice?

Prayer Prompts

DAY 1 （2） 3 4 5 6 7

WHEN WE PRAY "HALLOWED BE YOUR NAME":

- With reverence, we worship and honor God for His beauty and purity.

- We confess that we are broken and bruised. We give thanks for the great price Jesus paid, so that we can be in relationship with God who is holy.

- We desire to be more like Jesus. We ask to be filled with the Holy Spirit to have power to follow Jesus and be an advocate for His righteoussness in the world.

My Personal Prayers

Borrow the prayers that express what is in your heart, or add your own.

TO FATHER GOD   **TODAY IS** MM / DD / YY

PRAY SPOT ☐ Work   ☐ Home   ☐ School   ☐ _____

PATTERN HALLOWED BE YOUR NAME
PRIORITY WORSHIP OF YOU AS A HOLY GOD
REQUEST SHOW US WHO YOU ARE; FILL ME WITH AWE AND WONDER

MY LIFE

PONDERING YOUR HOLINESS, I FEEL:
☐
☐

I ADMIT I AM FAR FROM PERFECT; I AM NOT HOLY AS YOU ARE HOLY.
SHOW ME THE WAYS I HURT YOU AND HINDER MY RELATIONSHIP WITH YOU:
☐ I LIVE INDEPEDENTLY OF YOU, BUILDING MY OWN NAME AND GLORY.
☐ I HURT THE PEOPLE AROUND ME WITH HARSH WORDS OR ACTIONS.
☐
☐

THANK YOU FOR THE PRICE JESUS PAID FOR OUR UNRIGHTEOUSNESS.

My Personal Prayers

MY CITY

WHEN I LOOK AT MY CITY, I SEE PLACES WHERE RIGHTEOUSNESS IS NOT VALUED OR UPHELD, RESULTING IN DARK DEEDS. SHOW YOUR LIGHT IN THESE PLACES AND WORK OUT YOUR RIGHTEOUSNESS.

- ☐
- ☐

HOW DO YOU WANT ME TO BE AN ADVOCATE FOR RIGHTEOUSNESS IN THE WORLD AROUND ME?

- ☐ OPEN MY EYES TO SEE THE WAYS I CAN STAND FOR RIGHTEOUSNESS.
- ☐ GIVE ME COURAGE TO DO WHAT IS RIGHT.
- ☐
- ☐

My Personal Prayers

DAY 1 2 3 4 5 6 7

MY GRATITUDE

THANK YOU, GOD, FOR:

MY RESPONSE

NEW REVELATIONS, HEART CHANGES, OR STEPS I FEEL LED
BY YOU TO TAKE:

. . . in Jesus' Name, Amen

Your Kingdom Come

*"To clasp the hands in prayer
is the beginning of an uprising against
the disorder of the world."*
—Karl Barth

*"But that your prayer may have
its full weight with God,
see that ye be in charity with all men. . . .
Nor can you expect to receive any
blessing from God while you have not
charity towards your neighbor."*
—John Wesley

THE BIBLE'S CONCEPT OF KINGDOM IS RICH BUT NOT COMPLICATED. In its simplest sense, when Jesus tells us to pray "Your kingdom come," He emphasizes that we are to live our entire lives in light of His triumphant return, which will happen at the end of the world. No present suffering, discouragement, or opposition can overcome our confident hope that Jesus will soon restore all things. While we live our lives in the reality of the coming kingdom, we talk about, share, and proclaim the good news that Jesus has come, has finished the work of salvation, and is soon coming again.

But Jesus' kingdom does not come all at once. It comes in stages.

First, Jesus is our "Forever King." As part of the Trinity, Jesus has always ruled and reigned with the Father and Holy Spirit. When speaking of Christ, John states, "In the beginning was the Word, and the Word was with God, and the Word was God" (John 1:1).

Second, when Jesus lived and died for us, He became our "Redeemer King." Jesus is the King who accomplishes our salvation—His death was an inauguration, and His resurrection was a coronation. In Paul's letter to the Philippian Christians, Paul writes:

> And being found in appearance as a man, he humbled himself by becoming obedient to the point of death—even death on a cross! Therefore God exalted him to the highest place and gave him the name that is above every name, that at the name of Jesus every knee should bow, in heaven and on earth and under the earth, and every tongue acknowledge that Jesus Christ is Lord, to the glory of God the Father. (Phil. 2:8–11 NIV)

Third, Jesus is our "Coming King." He is the one who will judge and recreate all things at the end of the world. He promises that He will return, vindicate His faithful followers, and reveal the injustice of those who reject Him:

> They will see the Son of Man coming on the clouds of heaven with power and great glory. And he will send out his angels with a loud trumpet call, and they will gather his elect from the four winds, from one end of heaven to the other. (Matt. 24:30–31)

Jesus' kingdom is coming in a final sense because He is coming again to renew the entire creation and bring in the new age.

When we pray "Your kingdom come," we pray as loyal subjects who acknowledge His eternal creator-lordship. We pray as those who accept His saving work in His incarnation. We cry out in eager expectation of His coming again to renew all things.

A MODERN-DAY ILLUSTRATION

Living in a Western democracy, we may find it difficult to relate to the concept of living in a kingdom. But consider for a moment a modern parallel. Imagine a Fortune 500 company acquiring a smaller company that has fallen on hard times.

The buyer is Dominion Realty, a national corporation with offices and operations all over the country. Dominion buys out Independent Realty, a smaller outfit. The day after the acquisition, the Dominion CEO forms a transition team with these instructions: "You have three years to make Independent into a Dominion company. I do not want to chop this company up. I want to renew and rebuild it. Welcome in as many employees and managers as possible into our family. And call me any time you need me."

Dominion and Independent are in similar lines of work, but they have different cultures. Independent values individual accomplishments above everything, while Dominion is all about team work. At Independent, the philosophy is "pull your own weight, or you're dead weight." Whereas, the Dominion philosophy is "those we serve are as important as our team." Independent is concerned about the bottom line—Dominion is concerned about company culture.

Shortly after the acquisition, the transition team arrives on-site and gets to know Independent.

After a month of careful listening, they gather everyone together to make an announcement.

Corinne, the spokesperson, starts by stating the situation in simple terms: "You are going to become a Dominion company— nothing can stop that. But don't think for a minute we want to get rid of you! We want to win you over. Dominion is a great company with a great leader. If you are willing to get on board, you can be part of a fantastic future. If not, you will probably quit before we have to let you go. Bottom line, the CEO is coming soon. Our only job is to get ready for his coming."

> **During this interim period, we not only announce Jesus' coming, we teach, carry out, and model the plans of our coming King.**

We understand that, in this story, Jesus is the Dominion CEO. This world, insofar as it does not acknowledge His present lordship, is "Independent." The time between His first and second coming is the three-year transition. And Christians are the transition management team. Because of His finished work on the cross, Jesus defeated every enemy: sin, death, and the devil, and His second coming is unstoppable. It is our job to arrange everything and prepare for His coming.

During this interim period, we not only announce Jesus' coming, we teach, carry out, and model the plans of our coming King. Someone once said, "Christians are building show homes. Their job is to show what the new neighborhood will look like."

Let's return to our illustration.

At the outset, there are some who want nothing to do with the Dominion transformation. The Independent boss does not take long to make his views known:

"Everything we have worked so hard for is being ruined!"

Before long, he quits, sets up a competitor company, and takes some Independent staff with him.

However, other Independent employees are willing to take a look at Dominion. Most lived on long hours and low wages. They were constantly concerned about job security.

The Dominion team wants to reverse this trend. Peter, who is on the transition team, comes up to Jim, an account manager for Independent.

"Jim, I notice you let Frank go last week. Why? He seemed to be working hard."

Jim answers, "Yeah, he tried. But he couldn't cut it."

Peter reflects for a minute.

"Jim, I want you to give Frank another chance. Let's get him some training if he needs it. He seems to have a good attitude. I think we can make progress."

"Okay. You're the boss."

"Actually I'm not. I just work for him—like you!

"And by the way, Jim, I noticed you let six or seven others go in the past six months. I wonder if we shouldn't ask them back, too."

Eyebrows raised, Jim stares at Peter.

He asks, "I don't get it. What kind of company wants to keep everyone on payroll and even hire people back?"

Peter just smiles. He can see things from Jim's perspective.

"I understand. You see, it's our CEO. He likes to rebuild things. He likes to make winners out of losers." He continues, "When our boss was younger, he suffered what looked like a final defeat and humiliation. Everyone thought he was finished. No one gave him a chance. But somehow, he came back, stronger than ever. It happened suddenly—you might say miraculously. That's why he always gives second chances and third and fourth . . ."

Jim listens. "Interesting. But what about you?"

"I'm glad you ask. I was a workaholic, so bad that I lost my wife and my kids. Even my business went under. I was a useless wreck when, out of nowhere, the boss called me and welcomed me into his firm. He asked if I wanted to do some transition work. He thought I might be good at it. Now I get to help other shipwrecks like myself. And it feels good—really worthwhile."

"Okay, that makes some sense. But what about the others on

your team? What's their story?"

"Pretty much similar to mine. Corinne was forced to quit a high-paying job for a fast-food joint after leaving her abusive husband. Phil has terminal cancer. The boss offered him this job as a way to finish life on a high note. And here he is. Going out in a blaze of glory!"

Jim thought he saw tears welling up in Peter's eyes.

"You see, Jim, this is not just a job. Frankly, I love my boss. He could ask me to shovel manure and I would—in a minute!"

Jim didn't say anything.

He didn't know what to say.

SHARING OUR STORY

Taking our cue from Peter, we can understand a little more about Jesus' coming kingdom. Sharing what Jesus has done for us is not just a job. It's about loyalty to our coming King. While we wait for His return, we share our story. We explain to others how Jesus has established the kingdom of God once and for all.

We explain to anyone willing to listen—friends, relatives, colleagues—that God owns every last atom, proton, and electron in the universe. He is the all-powerful Creator-King, and every man, woman, and child owes Him worship and thanks (Rev. 5:13).

Some Christians feel that talking about the end of the world seems foreboding—even frightening. However, we need to remember this "ending" is a great beginning. All the history of this world is only a brief introduction, merely the cover of a book.

We haven't even gotten to the good stuff yet. In the rest of the story, sorrow, sickness, tears, and death will be left behind. What is weak becomes strong. Small fragments of precious faith are refined and perfected. Best of all, anyone who wants to start fresh and to live forever in unimaginable bliss alongside of God is welcome to become a part of His new world. We get to humbly pass out the invitations!

LIVING OUT THE VALUES OF THE KINGDOM

But there is more to the kingdom than sharing the story with others. We also ask for His grace and Spirit to live out the values and character of His coming kingdom today. We look for our present world to change as a result of His kingdom coming into our lives.

> While we wait for His return, we share our story. We explain to others how Jesus has established the kingdom of God once and for all.

Remember what the CEO says: "I want a Dominion company when I come back."

Dominion does not come in to end the doing of business! It comes, instead, to transform the way business is done.

This is true of Jesus' transition team, too. Though we have a new King, we live in the same communities, go to the same schools, and work in the same marketplace. We know "down-and-outers." We know "up-and-outers." We know "way-outers" too.

We are tasked with bringing the joy of God's kingdom to them, today. When we pray "Your kingdom come," we daily apply our prayers to the deep needs of our cities.

AN EXAMPLE IN VANCOUVER

In our city, a group of Christians helped found a public housing organization that works with local and civic leaders to help the impoverished and mentally ill by giving them the dignity of their own place to live.

The founding CEO came into this line of ministry after his family had to help one of its own members who struggled with mental illness. It took everything this family had to keep this loved one off the streets. Jesus used this time to prepare him for helping others in similar circumstances. This organization now serves hundreds of those struggling with mental illness or recovering from addictions. All are welcome. All are given the dignity of a home to live in.

> The outcome of genuine faith, and a genuine desire to see God's kingdom come, will always be a life of kindness, justice, and good works.

The founder put it this way: "Christians need to remember the great commandment as well as the great commission. Jesus taught us to love our neighbor as well as to lead him to faith." The theme verse of his life is from the prophet Isaiah:

> "Is not this the kind of fasting I have chosen. . . .
> Is it not to share your food with the hungry
>   and to provide the poor wanderer with shelter—
> when you see the naked, to clothe them,
>   and not to turn away from your own flesh and blood? . . .
> Your people will rebuild the ancient ruins
>   and will raise up the age-old foundations;
> you will be called Repairer of Broken Walls,
>   Restorer of Streets with Dwellings."
> (Isa. 58:6–7, 12 NIV)

The outcome of genuine faith, and a genuine desire to see God's kingdom come, will always be a life of kindness, justice, and good works.

THE ROLE OF PRAYER IN PREPARING FOR HIS COMING KINGDOM

Back to our story.

Jim from accounting is almost ready to join Dominion for good. He has one more important question to ask. He walks up to Peter and asks, "Tell me. Where do you get your energy and resolve to keep going? Frankly, I want some."

Peter smiles. "Jim, each of us has a direct line to the boss. If you want, you can have one too. He tells each of us to call him day or night for any reason whatsoever. He always answers. And he never seems in a rush. I can't remember him ever ending the conversation. When I have to say 'goodbye,' he says, 'Okay, but call back soon.'"

Like Peter, God's children have a direct line, too. It is prayer. We have unlimited personal and direct access to our Father for His friendship, strength, and wisdom. There is no obstacle that we cannot face with Him at our side. There is no challenge we cannot overcome by His grace and presence through prayer.

> The greatest joy of believers will be to see the face of Jesus when He comes in His glory. There will be no mistaking Him in that day.

POSTSCRIPT

At the end of three years, the CEO returns. Unannounced, he enters through the back. It is pretty obvious who he is. Everyone has been waiting for this day. As he goes through the offices, he starts to smile. He has a feel for things, and things feel good. Peter, Corrine, Ted, and Phil look excited and a bit nervous at the same time. Jim feels weak at the knees.

He gathers them together and, with a deep and genuine smile, says, "I like what I see. It feels like a Dominion company. I am really happy each of you is here. You are becoming a real team."

He turns to face Corrine and the other leaders. "Corrine, Peter, Ted, Phil—you have done it again! Good work. It's been a blast, hasn't it?"

He turns and looks at Jim. "Oh, and you, Jim. From the day I bought Independent, I knew you were going to be a part of us. Welcome home." He adds, "I want you to introduce share options for every employee. I want them to get a share of our success. This location is yours to run for me. Enjoy it. You have already proven you will do a great job."

I hope the point is clear. The greatest joy of believers will be to see the face of Jesus when He comes in His glory. There will be no mistaking Him in that day. We will be eager and anxious for Him to give His verdict on our work. When we pray "Your kingdom come," we pray to be ready for that day. We ask to hear, "Well done, good and faithful servant! You have been faithful with a few things; I will put you in charge of many things. Come and share your master's happiness!" (Matt. 25:23 NIV).

While we eagerly wait for the day of Jesus' coming, it is our highest privilege as God's children to let others know of Christ's return. The coming of the King is good news; indeed, it is the very best news. When the King returns, He brings salvation, joy, freedom, and forgiveness with Him.

> How beautiful upon the mountains
> are the feet of him who brings good news,
> who publishes peace, who brings good news of happiness,
> who publishes salvation,
> who says to Zion, "Your God reigns." (Isa. 52:7)

Some imagine that telling people about this good news is being pushy. This is a lie of the enemy who continues to conspire against the King and His people. How can inviting a friend, relative, neighbor, or colleague into a relationship with the King be anything but good? Grateful messengers are filled with the hope that many will accept this beautiful invitation of joy and happiness.

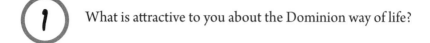
Prayerful Pondering

1   What is attractive to you about the Dominion way of life?

2   What is your view of the Dominion CEO, Jesus?

3   Which relationships or situations in the world around you might Jesus be asking you to represent His Dominion values—teamwork, transforming the way work is done, giving others a second, third, and fourth chance? What is one way you can do that this week?

Prayer Prompts

DAY   1   2   ③   4   5   6   7

WHEN WE PRAY, "YOUR KINGDOM COME":

- We give our loyalty to Jesus and seek His leadership in our lives.

- We ask for grace, wisdom, and courage to live out the values and character of Jesus' coming kingdom today.

- We cry out in eager expectation of Jesus coming again to renew all things. We pray for the deep needs of our city, for His values of restoration and rebuilding to reign.

DAY   1   2   ③   4   5   6   7

Borrow the prayers that express what is in your heart, or add your own.

TO   FATHER GOD   **TODAY IS**   MM / DD / YY

PRAYER SPOT: ☐ Work   ☐ Home   ☐ School   ☐ _____

PATTERN	YOUR KINGDOM COME
PRIORITY	SURRENDER TO YOUR LEADERSHIP & PURPOSES
REQUEST	LET YOUR WAYS BE ESTABLISHED

MY LIFE

I ADMIT IT'S HARD TO PRAY "YOUR KINGDOM COME" BECAUSE, IF I'M HONEST, MY INCLINATION IS TO LIVE FOR MYSELF AND BUILD MY OWN "KINGDOMS" IN DIFFERENT WAYS:

☐ ....

☐ ....

....

....

KNOWING THAT YOU WANT TO LEAD MY LIFE, I FEEL:

☐ ....

☐ ....

....

....

HELP ME SEE THE KIND OF LEADER YOU TRULY ARE.

My Personal Prayers

MY CITY

THANK YOU THAT YOU LOVE THE CITY. STRENGTHEN ITS FOUNDATION TO
BE BUILT ON YOUR VALUES. LET YOUR KINGDOM COME IN MY CITY, IN:

☐ THE NEIGHBORHOOD WHERE I LIVE

☐ THE COMMUNITY WHERE I WORK

☐

☐

BE PRESENT IN BROKEN AND DYSFUNCTIONAL PLACES:

☐ WHERE CONFLICT CAUSES DIVISION AND PAIN

☐ WHERE PEOPLE ARE SUFFERING HARDSHIP OR INJUSTICE

☐

☐

LET YOUR LIGHT SHINE STRONGER THAN THE DARKNESS &
CHALLENGES. RESTORE & RENEW THE CITY AND THE PEOPLE —
BECAUSE OF HOW YOU LOVE THEM.

My Personal Prayers

DAY   1   2   ③   4   5   6   7

- [ ] GIVE ME YOUR HEART THAT CARES ENOUGH TO ENGAGE
- [ ] GIVE ME COURAGE AND WISDOM TO BUILD UP PEOPLE & MY CITY
- [ ]
- [ ]

MY GRATITUDE

THANK YOU, FATHER, FOR:

MY RESPONSE

NEW REVELATIONS, THOUGHTS, HEART CHANGES, OR STEPS I
FEEL COMPELLED BY YOU TO TAKE:

. . . in Jesus' Name, Amen

Your Will Be Done on Earth as It Is in Heaven

"Prayer is a mighty instrument,
not for getting man's will done in heaven,
but for getting God's will done on earth."
—Robert Law

"Prayer does not blind us to the world,
but it transforms our vision of the world,
and makes us see it . . . in the light of God."
—Thomas Merton

GOD'S WILL IS RICH, DEEP, AND MULTIFACETED. In its most comprehensive sense, God's will is the environment within which all creatures exist. When Jesus asserts that God's will is "done in heaven," He means that God's will is the symphony to which all heaven and its myriad angelic hosts are tuned. This music is so vast and deep and rich that all the songs of heaven are a part of it. God created the world "while the morning stars sang together and all the angels shouted for joy" (Job 38:7 NIV). Think of the world's great symphonies—*The Planets*, the *Pastoral* Symphony, *The Four Seasons*. Throw in Clarke's *Trumpet Voluntary* and imagine them all rolled into one harmonious, beautiful, and joyous song.

We are to do God's will on earth "as in heaven" because God's thousands upon thousands of angels in heaven are in perfect harmony with God's will (Heb. 12:22 NIV). The cherubim— awesome angelic beings who surround God's throne—are so tuned to God's will that their very movements are in sync with God. "Wherever the Spirit would go, they would go" (Ezek. 1:20 NIV).

If we are to carry out God's will on earth as it is in heaven, it is more than a matter of simple obedience. We need to share the angels' inner harmony with the will of God. Our wills need to be tuned to God's will. This is the transformational goal of this command (Rom. 12:2).

Yet the reality is that we constantly see activity "on earth" that is clearly contrary to His will. From earliest history, there is a dissonance on earth because we have edited God out from the songs of our lives. This dissonance manifests itself as exploitation, propaganda, violence, cruelty, and all other forms of injustice. It has spread through all places through all history.

Yet God does not surrender His song to this discord. He renews the concert of His will— His perfect plan and purpose—to center stage in history. When Jesus comes to the stable in Bethlehem, we hear heaven's music on earth once again:

> **From earliest history, there is a dissonance on earth because we have edited God out from the songs of our lives.**

Suddenly a great company of the heavenly host appeared with the angel, praising God and saying, "Glory to God in the highest heaven, and on earth peace to those on whom his favor rests." (Luke 2:13–14 NIV)

When Jesus surrenders His life on a Roman cross, we imagine a song of lament, a funeral eulogy, as the earth itself groans and the skies mourn in darkness. This song is so heartrending and sorrowful that to hear it is to remember it forever.

When Jesus rises from the dead, we spring from the minor key. We hear the pizzicato of the strings, the dance of the woodwinds, and uproarious thunder of the percussion. Our hearts leap and creation dances to the triumphant chorus. This song spreads in overwhelming joy and healing "as far as the curse is found" (*Joy to the World*).

Oh sing to the LORD a new song;
sing to the LORD, all the earth!
   Sing to the LORD, bless his name;
tell of his salvation from day to day. . . .
   Let the heavens be glad, and let the earth rejoice;
let the sea roar, and all that fills it;
   let the field exult, and everything in it!
Then shall all the trees of the forest sing for joy
   before the LORD, for he comes,
   for he comes to judge the earth.
   He will judge the world in righteousness,
and the peoples in his faithfulness.
   (Ps. 96:1–2, 11–13)

When we pray, "Your will be done on earth as it is in heaven,"
we are asking to once again hear the symphony of God's will. We
want to tune our lives to this music and to become a joyous part
of its song. We want to obey God, but we want to do it with a
song of joy and thanks in our heart.

THE SCOPE OF THIS PRAYER

When we ask that "your will be done on earth as it is in heaven,"
we pray for at least three things. First, we ask to accept God's
will. Second, we pray to approve God's will. Third, we pray to do
God's will.

FIRST WE PRAY TO ACCEPT GOD'S WILL

God's will is done—always and everywhere. To try to live
outside God's will is impossible. His will permeates all existence.
In one sense, to oppose God's will is futile. We cannot break
God's will—in the sense of preventing Him from doing what He

decides to do. We can only be broken in the attempt.

An ancient pagan king of Babylon named Nebuchadnezzar found out about God's unbreakable will the hard way. One day he decides to take credit for his kingdom's success and glory. As he walks the palace walls and surveys Babylon and all its splendors—perhaps looking at the hanging gardens—he boasts: "Is not this great Babylon, which I have built by my mighty power as a royal residence and for the glory of my majesty?" (Dan. 4:30).

For this pride, God stripped Nebuchadnezzar of his throne and made him crawl on all fours until his hair looked like eagle's feathers and his nails like bird's claws. When he finally wakes up to his folly, the first thing he proclaims throughout his kingdom is that God is sovereign overall and nothing and no one can stop God from doing what He chooses to do:

> When we pray, "Your will be done on earth as it is in heaven," we are asking to once again hear the symphony of God's will.

for his dominion is an everlasting dominion,
  and his kingdom endures from generation to generation;
all the inhabitants of the earth are accounted as nothing,
  and he does according to his will among the host of heaven
  and among the inhabitants of the earth;
and none can stay his hand
  or say to him, "What have you done?" (Dan. 4:34–35)

Therefore, when we pray "Your will be done," we affirm that God's rule and reign extends everywhere. We accept the limitation of our freedom when we pray "Your will be done." Only God is absolutely free and undetermined. As Psalm 115 states, "Our God is in the heavens; he does all that he pleases" (v. 3).

Everything in heaven and earth is created, and God alone is Creator. Every creature is dependent on the Creator—He stands above the creation in His self-determination and freedom. Our freedom is limited by our nature, our environment, and by God's plan and purposes.

Therefore, when we pray "Your will be done," we worship God and ensure that all of our plans and purposes begin and end with *Deo volente*—"God willing."

SECOND, WE ASK TO APPROVE GOD'S WILL

When we accept God's will, we do not just resign ourselves to it. God's will is not fate. His will is a living expression of His being and reveals His wisdom, justice, and truth. Once we get to know God's will and to accept it, we soon learn to approve it: "Do not be conformed to this world, but be transformed by the renewing of your mind, that by testing you may discern what is the will of God, what is good and acceptable and perfect" (Rom. 12:2).

Approving God's will is not always easy. Consider how the biblical character Job interprets God's will. Catastrophe strikes Job from all sides. Simultaneously, he loses his property to looters, his animals to fire, and his children to a freak storm. What Job says in response to the catastrophe reveals that he accepts and approves God's will:

> Then Job arose and tore his robe and shaved his head and fell on the ground and worshiped. And he said, "Naked I came from my mother's womb, and naked shall I return. The LORD gave, and the LORD has taken away; blessed be the name of the LORD."
> In all this Job did not sin or charge God with wrong. (Job 1:20–22)

This is not resignation. Job does not believe in fate. He knows that God's will is over every event of his life. He knows that God is not capricious or malicious, in spite of how circumstances appear. He believes that God has a higher purpose, even if Job cannot discern it.

Nor does Job believe he is being punished for his sins. He lives by grace and not by karma. When his "friends" insist that he is getting what he deserves because of his many sins, Job maintains that God is not judging him as an offender but is testing him as His child. To that end, he refuses to characterize God as a heartless judge. This is the main theme of Job. He knows that Satan's tempting is God's testing.

This is important. When we pray "Your will be done," we are asking to understand and approve God's will—especially in the hard times.

The best example of accepting and approving of God's will is Jesus Christ Himself. In His final days on earth, Jesus is in the garden of Gethsemane. He knows what agony is in store for Him at the cross. He knows that He will be cruelly murdered. He already feels the burden of mankind's sin. In this terrible moment, Jesus does not just wrestle with fate. In prayer, He struggles with, and within, the will of God:

> Then he said to them, "My soul is overwhelmed with sorrow to the point of death. Stay here and keep watch with me."
>
> Going a little farther, he fell with his face to the ground and prayed, "My Father, if it is possible, may this cup be taken from me. Yet not as I will, but as you will." (Matt. 26:38–39 NIV)

Jesus' sorrow is real, and His pain is intense, yet He realizes that His heavenly Father permits His suffering for the highest of purposes—the salvation of the universe!

In the same way, the key to our growth in grace is to pray to approve of God's will for our lives: "I cry out to God Most High, to God who fulfills his purpose for me" (Ps. 57:2).

In believing prayer, we learn to connect our present troubles to the good and perfect will of God. We refuse to believe that chance rules our lives. We withstand the temptation to imagine that God is capricious or malicious. We know He has a higher purpose and that He is not dealing with us as our sins deserve. Listen to what Peter the apostle says about God's higher purposes:

> Dear friends, do not be surprised at the fiery ordeal that has come on you to test you, as though something strange were happening to you. But rejoice inasmuch as you participate in the sufferings of Christ, so that you may be overjoyed when his glory is revealed. If you are insulted because of the name of Christ, you are blessed, for the Spirit of glory and of God rests on you. . . . However, if you suffer as a Christian, do not be ashamed, but praise God that you bear that name. . . .
>
> So then, those who suffer according to God's will should commit themselves to their faithful Creator and continue to do good. (1 Peter 4:12–14, 16, 19 NIV)

As we bring our troubles to Jesus in prayer—asking His will to be done—we approve the will of our Father in heaven. We see our sufferings in the greater reality of His good, acceptable, and perfect will. In prayer we "turn crisis to Christ." Our heart becomes tuned to His heart, and we sing the song of grace.

This is good news when it comes to prayer! Once we learn to accept and approve of God's will, we are able to pray with great effect and assurance. When we ask according to God's will, our will is tuned and in harmony with His will. We not only know God's will from the Bible, we have learned to approve His will from our spiritual growth and experience. Jesus calls this harmony with God's will "abiding."

> I am the vine; you are the branches. . . . If you abide in me, and my words abide in you, ask whatever you wish, and it will be done for you. By this my Father is glorified, that you bear much fruit and so prove to be my disciples. (John 15:5, 7–8)

Those who abide in Jesus learn to pray according to God's will and have an inner assurance that their prayers are answered.

THIRD, WE PRAY TO DO GOD'S WILL ON EARTH AS IN HEAVEN

God's will is perfect. His will is unchangeable and is as living and alive as God is. In order to make His will clear, God has given us commands as a rule and guide for life. He requires our obedience to His laws.

Once again, heaven is our example. The chief joy of the angels is to obey God's commands. In fact, we have no biblical examples of angels acting independently of God's commands:

> The LORD has established his throne in the heavens,
> and his kingdom rules over all.
> Bless the LORD, O you his angels,
> you mighty ones who do his word,

In believing prayer, we learn to connect our present troubles to the good and perfect will of God.

obeying the voice of his word!
Bless the LORD, all his hosts,
his ministers, who do his will! (Ps. 103:19–21)

For us to pray and do God's will "as in heaven," we are not to
obey God grudgingly but to rejoice in obeying God.

God's commands are more than rules. Rules are simply legal
boundaries and are impersonal. Consider sporting events: The
referee who executes the rules does not have to feel passionate
about them. God's commands, in contrast, are not just rules.
They express His holy character. They express His identity. God
is not a disinterested referee who just makes sure the game is
kept "in hand." He is passionate about His laws—for them to be
kept—from the heart.

God's will includes a passion for justice. His will includes grief
and sorrow for victims of injustice. To do God's will, in its fullest
sense, is more than mere obedience. True obedience includes
sharing His passion for justice and His compassion for victims of
injustice. God is internally committed to justice. In fact, justice
is an attribute of God. His laws are supremely just. He appoints
those who have authority in family, society, and church to
maintain justice and stop oppression.

Cruelty and injustice happen every day in every city. Women
and children are molested. Many people are physically abused
in their own homes. Innocent parties are left in ruins after ugly
divorce battles. Immigrants are subject to prejudice and given
demeaning work. The mentally ill are sent out of crowded
hospitals and left to fend for themselves on the streets. From
their deepest heart, each victim cries questions of anguish: "Is
my suffering God's will? Does God care? Is there justice? Will
God rescue me from my oppressor?"

When we ask to do God's will, we commit to listen to these

kinds of questions. We ask to know and to share God's passion for justice and His grief at injustice. We pray to hear the cries of the victim and ask to be willing to be the answer. Our prayer for God's will, therefore, is effective only if we share God's love of justice and hatred of oppression, exploitation, and violence.

DEEDS ARE AN OUTCOME OF PRAYER

It is not enough to just know God's will or to pray for God's will to be done, we need grace and courage to obey and carry it out. The rubber has to hit the road. This is the "earth" where Jesus' will is to be done.

When we pray, "Your will be done on earth as it is in heaven," we are committing to doing God's will. Facing the enormous social problems in our cities today, we do not say, "What has this got to do with me? This is the government's job." We cannot say, "This is not my problem. This is part of the wickedness of the world. I am separate from that. I have to protect and preserve my righteousness." Instead we pray, "Your will be done in me and through me." We pray for wisdom and courage to get involved in our city. God gives us wisdom. He will raise up leaders and servants to do His will.

During the years I served as a pastor, our church committed to practically respond to the Lord's Prayer by working alongside different ministry programs. One of which we helped establish is called Showers for the Shelterless. In this program, we partnered with others in our community to serve the homeless and mentally ill. Guests are greeted by someone who cares for their shopping carts and dogs, while they enjoy coffee, breakfast, and a newspaper as they await their shower. We have the privilege to visit, serve, and get to know them.

Under the leadership of Genesis Vancouver, now known as

SA Foundation, we prayed for and find practical ways to support this wonderful outreach that ministers to sexually exploited women and their children. We prayed that God would deliver those exploited not only from pimps and "Johns" but also from a culture that exploits us all. We partnered and prayed for Genesis Vancouver to provide safe houses and day programs for the sexually exploited and their children.

There is a connection between our praying for justice and justice coming to pass. Speaking to the people of Israel while exiled in Babylon, Jeremiah reminds them to seek justice for their city:

"Also, seek the peace and prosperity of the city to which I carried you in exile. Pray to the LORD for it, because if it prospers, you too will prosper. . . . For I know the plans I have for you," declares the LORD, "plans to prosper you and not to harm you, plans to give you hope and a future. Then you will call on me and come and pray to me, and I will listen to you." (Jer. 29:7, 11–12 NIV)

Notice how prayer for the city is commanded and how God promises He will answer with peace and prosperity.

Let's take another look at the striking passage in Isaiah 58. As in Jeremiah, there is a connection between our prayers for urban renewal[3] and God's promise to hear this prayer. However, something crucial is added. God's answer to our prayer is that He sends us into the city to be His agents of transformation. He will rebuild the city. He will do it through those who pray. We become the answer to our own prayer!

> "Is not this the kind of fasting I have chosen:
>   to loose the chains of injustice
>   and untie the cords of the yoke,
>   to set the oppressed free
>   and break every yoke?
>   Is it not to share your food with the hungry
>   and to provide the poor wanderer with shelter—
>   when you see the naked, to clothe them,
>   and not to turn away from your own flesh and blood?
>   Then your light will break forth like the dawn,
>   and your healing will quickly appear;
>   then your righteousness will go before you,
>   and the glory of the LORD will be your rear guard.
>   Then you will call, and the LORD will answer;
>   you will cry for help, and he will say: Here am I. . . .
>   Your people will rebuild the ancient ruins
>   and will raise up the age-old foundations;
>   you will be called Repairer of Broken Walls,
>   Restorer of Streets with Dwellings." (Isa. 58:6–9, 12 NIV)

The implication is clear. As God's people, we are to pray for His will to be done on earth.

God cares deeply for the city and all who dwell there (Jonah 4:10–11). We are to become deeply engaged with the needs of our surrounding community. God will answer our prayer as we do so—He will rescue the needy and establish safe neighborhoods. The way God renews the city is by sending His people to carry out this mandate. This is how His will is done "on earth as it is in heaven."

Let it sink in. Let it take your breath away. As we seek God's will in prayer, and then carry it out, we will embody the transformation the oppressed cry out for! We will see substantial healing and restoration at the heart of our city. What a marvelous encouragement to pray.

> **As we seek God's will in prayer, and then carry it out, we will embody the transformation the oppressed cry out for!**

Prayerful Pondering

1 How open is your heart to tuning in and hearing the symphony of God's will for your life?

2 When you look at the world around you, where do you feel and see the dissonance of injustice?

3 Where might God be asking you to pray for and engage with the needs around you, to be involved in His will to renew and restore the city and its people? How willing are you to be the answer to your prayers?

Prayer Prompts

WHEN WE PRAY, "YOUR WILL BE DONE ON EARTH AS IT IS IN HEAVEN":

- We surrender and ask for our will to be in harmony with, and to do, God's will.

- We pray to hear the cry of the victim. We pray for passion for justice, for compassion, and rehabilitation of both the victims and offenders.

- We ask to be willing to carry out His will on earth. We pray for courage and wisdom to get involved in the needs of our city.

Try praying through the newspaper one day this week. Ask God to show you His perspective and heart for the people, places, and problems that are in your city and world. Pray for His will to be done.

Prayerful Pondering

DAY   1   2   3   (4)   5   6   7

Borrow the prayers that express what is in your heart, or add your own.

TO   FATHER GOD   **TODAY IS**   MM / DD / YY

PRAYER SPOT: Work   Home   School   _____

PATTERN   YOUR WILL BE DONE ON EARTH AS IT IS IN HEAVEN

PRIORITY   KNOWING YOUR WILL OF COMPASSION AND JUSTICE

REQUEST   REVEAL AND FULFILL YOUR GOOD WILL AND PLEASURE

MY LIFE

THANK YOU, JESUS, THAT YOU KNOW WHAT IT'S LIKE TO STRUGGLE
WITH YOUR FATHER'S WILL. I ASK FOR YOUR WILL TO BE DONE
SPECIFICALLY IN THE AREA OF:

☐ MY CAREER

☐ MY RELATIONSHIPS

☐ A SPECIFIC DECISION

☐

☐

YOUR WILL CAN BE SO DIFFERENT THAN MY WILL:

☐ HELP ME TO UNDERSTAND WHAT YOUR WILL IS

☐ GIVE ME WILLINGNESS TO TRUST AND DESIRE YOUR WILL

☐

☐

My Personal Prayers

MY CITY

LET YOUR WILL BE DONE IN MY CITY AS IT IS IN HEAVEN.
WHEN I THINK OF ALL THE CITY'S NEEDS AND PROBLEMS, I FEEL:

☐ HOPEFUL   ☐ UNSURE   ☐ EXCITED   ☐ OVERWHELMED
☐   ☐
☐   ☐

I PRAY FOR YOUR WILL TO BE DONE IN THE AREAS WHERE IT SEEMS
LIKE YOUR GOOD WILL, JUSTICE, AND MERCY ARE FAR FROM PRESENT:

☐ WHERE THE POOR AND DISADVANTAGED ARE EXPLOITED OR NEGLECTED
☐ WHERE GREED LEADS TO CORRUPTION
☐
☐

GIVE ME WISDOM TO KNOW THE SPECIFIC NEEDS IN MY CITY AND OF MY
NEIGHBORS WHERE YOU WANT ME TO PARTICIPATE IN BRINGING YOUR

☐ MERCY   ☐ COMPASSION   ☐ HOPE   ☐

SHOW ME PRACTICAL WAYS AND GIVE ME OPPORTUNITIES TO LOVE MY
NEIGHBORS AND CITY AS JESUS WOULD WITH COMPASSION.

☐
☐

My Personal Prayers

DAY   1   2   3   (4)   5   6   7

MY GRATITUDE

THANK YOU, FATHER, FOR:

MY RESPONSE

NEW REVELATIONS, THOUGHTS, HEART CHANGES, OR STEPS I FEEL
COMPELLED BY YOU TO TAKE:

. . . in Jesus' Name, Amen

Give Us This Day Our Daily Bread

"Earthly riches are full of poverty."
—St. Augustine

"'I experienced today the most exquisite pleasure
I ever had in my life,' said a young invalid;
'I was able to breathe freely for above five minutes.'"
—J. Oswald Sanders

"Life cannot be satisfied
when it is lived out as a consuming entity."
—Ravi Zacharias

"GIVE US THIS DAY OUR DAILY BREAD" IS A SIMPLE PHRASE THAT SUMMARIZES ALL OUR PRAYERS FOR EARTHLY CONCERNS.

"Bread" is more than food. It also refers to the Word of God. Jesus said, "Man shall not live by bread alone, but by every word that comes from the mouth of God" (Matt. 4:4). Bread refers to the enjoyment of the gospel and faith in God.

It is also a metaphor for all of life's necessities. When we ask for daily bread, we also ask for propitious weather for our crops, for honest government to oversee equitable distribution to rich and poor alike, and for good health so that we can enjoy our food. Robert Burns once said a prayer:[4]

> Some have meat and cannot eat,
>> And some cannot eat that want it.
> But we have meat, and we can eat,
>> So let the Lord be thankit.

When we pray for daily bread, our request has a specific meaning as well as a comprehensive application. We are asking for all of life's necessities as well as the peace and health to enjoy them.

ASKING FOR DAILY BREAD SLOWLY CHANGES OUR ENTIRE OUTLOOK ON LIFE

As we pray this amazing prayer, we not only receive what we ask for—bread—we also discover that Jesus is transforming us. First, He is teaching us trust and thankfulness. Second, He is building in us generosity and kindness. Third, Jesus is developing contentment and an appreciation for the simplicity of life in us. We become what we pray.

1. AS WE PRAY, WE LEARN TRUST AND THANKFULNESS

When we humbly ask, "Give us this day our daily bread," we acknowledge that all good things come from God. When we credit our own labor and industry for the prosperity we enjoy, we are denying that life is a gift.

In Canada, a wealthy person puts in a long day to make a good living. In Kolkata, a rickshaw driver works day and night to make a few rupees. If a person is poor, it often has nothing to do with how industrious he is. He or she may not have the opportunity to make a good living.

When we pray for bread, we lift up empty hands, and in humble thankfulness, we acknowledge that all good things we enjoy come from God. We depend on God to fill all our needs from His own bounty and kindness. Asking for daily bread involves turning from self-reliance and asking for a heart that relies on God.

TRUST IN GOD'S PROVISION IS ENRICHED WITH THANKFULNESS OF HEART

The habit of asking implies a response of thanksgiving. There is no greater proof of Jesus' work in our hearts than genuine thankfulness. Thanksgiving is an antidote to greed and to envy. When we give thanks, we take our eyes off of what we do not have.

Just as the world looks smaller from the window of a plane at 35,000 feet, in thankful prayer, we rise above daily problems and see the abundance of God. It is amazing how discontent with bills, mortgage, and the expenses of life disappears when we give thanks for the abundance on our table each day.

> **When we pray for bread, we lift up empty hands, and in humble thankfulness, we acknowledge that all good things we enjoy come from God.**

Achieving thankfulness is at the heart of Jesus' plan for His people. When the Israelites returned from the Babylonian captivity and rebuilt the city walls, their leaders "appointed two great choirs that gave thanks" (Neh. 12:31).

To the believers at Philippi, Paul explains how thankfulness cures worry:

> Do not be anxious about anything, but in everything by prayer and supplication with thanksgiving let your requests be made known to God. And the peace of God, which surpasses all understanding, will guard your hearts and your minds in Christ Jesus. (Phil. 4:6–7)

As we pray, we move from anxiety and restlessness about possessions to a spirit of "joyfully giving thanks." When we start our day or begin a meal with simple thankfulness, we are cultivating an attitude of contentment and inner joy.

2. AS WE PRAY, WE LEARN KINDNESS AND GENEROSITY

We do not ask, "give *me* this day *my* daily bread." We pray, "give us this day our daily bread." This is a prayer for others as much as it is a prayer for ourselves. We pray for our friends, neighbors, family—indeed, our country and whole world—to have daily bread. As we love our neighbor in prayer, we are also to love our neighbor in deeds:

> If anyone has material possessions and sees a brother or sister in need but has no pity on them, how can the love of God be in that person? . . .
> Whoever claims to love God yet hates a brother or sister is a liar. For whoever does not love their brother and sister, whom they have seen, cannot love God, whom they have not seen. (1 John 3:17; 4:20 NIV)

Jesus' parable of the good Samaritan in Luke 10 teaches us never to discriminate when it comes to compassion and kindness. In the parable, there is a wounded and naked Jewish man on the roadside in need of help. While Jewish religious individuals intentionally walk on the other side of the road to avoid him, the Samaritan—whose people were sworn enemies of the Jews—bandages and feeds his enemy. This foreigner's love for God is evidenced by his compassion.

WHEN WE PRAY THIS PRAYER, WE ASK FOR A GENEROUS SPIRIT

When we ask for daily bread, we ask for the ability and willingness to give an increasing portion of what we have to others in need. Jesus says, "Freely you have received. Freely give." No matter how much we make or own, we ask to be content with a modest portion. We pray for courage and integrity to give sacrificially to Christ's mission and to those in need.

Christian giving is sacrificial because it is modeled after the sacrifice of Jesus: "For you know the grace of our Lord Jesus Christ, that though he was rich, yet for your sake he became poor, so that you by his poverty might become rich" (2 Cor. 8:9). Jesus not only sets the perfect standard for generosity, He also points to an "out of the way" gift of a widow to illustrate Christian giving:

> **When we ask for daily bread, we ask for the ability and willingness to give an increasing portion of what we have to others in need.**

> Jesus looked up and saw the rich putting their gifts into the offering box, and he saw a poor widow put in two small copper coins. And he said, "Truly, I tell you, this poor widow has put in more than all of them. For they all contributed out of their abundance, but she out of her poverty put in all she had to live on." (Luke 21:1–4)

Tithing is a good habit and guideline (some are not able to give more), but Jesus' example and teaching calls for each one to give to the church and the poor with sacrificial generosity. The early church followed Jesus' teaching when they exceeded giving guidelines by sharing all they had, so there would be equality among them and no one would be lacking any material needs (Acts 2:42–47).

Jesus says, "Love your neighbor as yourself." This means we should love and care for our neighbors as much as we care for ourselves. Life is meant to be lived in balance. Our life is a balance of three relationships—God, others, and self. A mature believer balances and prioritizes his or her time, energy, and resources on God first, others second, and self third.

However, anything near this balance is rare. On average, each of us spends more than 95% of life's income on ourselves.[5] No matter how we slice it, this is not a life of balance. There is too little left for God and others. This lack of balance leads to ill health and a poor state of mind. We can trace a good deal of spiritual unhappiness and discontent to a preoccupation with self.

As we follow Jesus in day-by-day prayer for bread, God will lead us to a life of kindness and generosity—to a life of balance.

3. AS WE PRAY, WE LEARN CONTENTMENT AND SIMPLICITY

When we ask God for "this day's" bread, we seek God's provision one day at a time. We leave tomorrow to Him.

This is what the lesson of the manna teaches in Exodus 16.

The children of Israel are led through the wilderness for forty years. God provides them with daily bread, called manna. It contains everything they need in the way of nourishment. However, it only lasts that day and rots overnight.

> When we ask "this day" for bread, we ask for a portion of life's blessings that is enough for this day.

God provides His children a lesson of daily trust in this. He teaches the Israelites to look to Him one day at a time for all they need and not to store up in fear of tomorrow, but rely on Him for today. When we ask "this day" for bread, we ask for a portion of life's blessings that is enough for this day. We do not ask for too little—so that we are unable pay our bills, provide for our dependents, and help those in need. Rather, we ask for just enough.

We may have savings accounts, insurance, and retirement plans, but if we are not careful these "storehouses" become a substitute for daily reliance upon God! Jesus tells us a simple and powerful parable about this "storehouse" problem:

> "The ground of a certain rich man yielded an abundant harvest. He thought to himself, 'What shall I do? I have no place to store my crops.'
>
> Then he said, 'This is what I'll do. I will tear down my barns and build bigger ones, and there I will store my surplus grain. And I'll say to myself, "You have plenty of grain laid up for many years. Take life easy; eat, drink and be merry."' But God said to him, 'You fool! This very night your life will be demanded from you. Then who will get what you have prepared for yourself?'
>
> This is how it will be with whoever stores up things for themselves but is not rich toward God." (Luke 12:16–21 NIV)

There is wisdom in planning for retirement, but when we pay more attention to our savings than to God, we are like the rich fool. This rich man trusted in his own industry and plans to make his future secure. Jesus is telling us to repent of self-reliance, and rather to trust God for everything we need and daily provision. Instead of fixating on our savings—we are to train our hearts in thankful worship.

When we ask for daily bread, we leave it in God's hands to decide how much or how little is right for us. He can take us through times of want and scarcity and times of plenty. God knows what each of His children can handle. He knows what we need and how much we need. He has a perfect plan for us. Poverty or riches is not the issue—contentment is. Just look, He says, at the world He has created:

> "Therefore I tell you, do not worry about your life, what you will eat or drink; or about your body, what you will wear. . . . Look at the birds of the air; they do not sow or reap or store away in barns, and yet your heavenly Father feeds them. Are you not much more valuable than they? Can any one of you by worrying add a single hour to your life?
>
> "And why do you worry about clothes? See how the flowers of the field grow. They do not labor or spin. Yet I tell you that not even Solomon in all his splendor was dressed like one of these. . . . But seek first his kingdom and his righteousness, and all these things will be given to you as well. Therefore do not worry about tomorrow, for tomorrow will worry about itself. Each day has enough trouble of its own." (Matt. 6:25–29, 33–34 NIV)

Each time I pray this prayer for daily bread, I take time to thank God for the various kinds of "daily bread" I enjoy. I ask God to help me to trust Him one day at a time and to forgive and still my restless desire to store up for tomorrow.

ASKING FOR "BREAD" ENCOURAGES A LIFE OF SIMPLICITY

Bread is wonderful. Walk into any bakery early in the morning and you know what I mean. The aroma stirs every hungry cell.

Yet bread is the simplest of foods.

In this petition, we ask to live with increasing simplicity. Simplicity is difficult for us. When we sell a house at a good profit, inherit some money, or receive a raise or bonus, without thinking, we immediately plan how to spend or save it. We make our lives more cluttered than before! In our aptly named "consumer culture," this habit of increased acquisition seems obvious and right. In contrast, Jesus' call to simplicity seems quaint or absurd.

However, following Jesus and praying this prayer has radical consequences. Simplicity becomes a beautiful thing. In contrast, living for luxury and self-indulgence becomes ugly. It takes something overwhelmingly beautiful to expel the shallow facsimile.

Prayerful Pondering

1   What are you thankful for today?

2   How much are your heart and life characterized by contentment? In what ways do you struggle with anxiety, self-indulgence, or desire for accumulating more?

3   How much of your time/talent/treasure are you storing and spending on yourself? How much are you sharing with others? With God?

Prayer Prompts

WHEN WE PRAY FOR "OUR DAILY BREAD":

- We thank God for all that we have, recognizing it all as a grace from Him. We ask for a spirit of gratitude and contentment, simplicity in our living, and generosity with what He has given us.

- We ask God to provide for our earthly needs. We confess our anxieties and our self-sufficiency. We ask for a heart that trusts and relies on God.

- We pray for our country and world to have daily bread. We ask for just rulers, honest government, wisdom for public leaders, educators, and policy makers, as well as peace and health to enjoy life's many necessities and blessings.

Prayer Practice

Spend some time in thanksgiving and praise. Write your own gratitude list. Taking time during meals is an easy place to start.

My Personal Prayers

Borrow the prayers that express what is in your heart, or add your own.

TO *FATHER GOD*   **TODAY IS** MM / DD / YY

PRAYER SPOT: Work   Home   School   _____

PATTERN   GIVE US THIS DAY OUR DAILY BREAD

PRIORITY   TRUSTING YOU AS PROVIDER FOR TODAY'S NEEDS

REQUEST   MAY WE LIVE SIMPLY AND CONTENTED WITH WHAT YOU GIVE US THAT WE MAY SHARE GENEROUSLY WITH OTHERS

MY LIFE

WHEN I PAUSE TO THINK ABOUT IT, YOU HAVE BEEN SO GENEROUS TO ME. THANK YOU FOR THE MANY KINDS OF "DAILY BREAD" YOU PROVIDE:

☐

☐

My Personal Prayers

EVEN WITH THIS ABUNDANCE, I ADMIT MY FOCUS CAN INSTEAD BE ON LUSTING AFTER WHAT I DO NOT HAVE BECAUSE OF:

☐ MY DESIRE FOR COMFORT & PLEASURE

☐ TRYING TO SAVE TOO FAR AHEAD BECAUSE I LIKE HAVING SECURITY/CONTROL

☐

☐

YOU ALREADY KNOW ALL MY NEEDS AND HOW TO BEST MEET THEM.

☐ HELP ME TO TRUST YOU TO PROVIDE FOR MY SPECIFIC NEEDS

☐ GIVE ME GRATITUDE, CONTENTMENT, SIMPLICITY, AND GENEROSITY

☐

☐

MY CITY

I PRAY THAT YOU WOULD MEET THE NEEDS OF MY CITY:

☐

☐

My Personal Prayers

DAY 1 2 3 4 (5) 6 7

MY RESPONSE

TEACH ME TO BE A WISE MANAGER OF ALL YOU'VE GIVEN ME. WHAT
PRACTICAL WAYS ARE YOU ASKING ME TO INVEST TO EXTEND YOUR
GRACE & BLESSING TO PEOPLE IN MY LIFE & CITY?

☐ MY TIME, ENERGY & ABILITIES

☐ MY TREASURES & MATERIAL WEALTH

MY GRATITUDE

THANK YOU, FATHER, FOR:

MY RESPONSE

NEW REVELATIONS, THOUGHTS, HEART CHANGES, OR STEPS I FEEL
COMPELLED BY YOU TO TAKE:

. . . in Jesus' Name, Amen

Forgive Us Our Debts as We Also Have Forgiven Our Debtors

"Criticism of others nails them to the past.
Prayer for them releases them into the future."
—Frank Laubach

"We cannot be wrong with man and right with God."
—The Kneeling Christian

IT IS CURIOUS THAT JESUS LEAVES THIS URGENT NECESSITY TOWARD THE END OF HIS PRAYER. Why did He not start with forgiveness?

In His prayer, Jesus puts God first. He teaches us to do the same. Jesus also wants us to know how to approach God, so we know what to ask forgiveness for. "Our Father" sets the relational context, which permits a humble, confident approach to God—faults and all. If we do not come to God as Father, we will tend to approach Him as a forbidding judge.

WHAT NEEDS TO BE FORGIVEN

We need to be forgiven for our sins. But what is sin? There is no easy answer to this question. Philosopher Seneca the Younger said, "Devotion to what is wrong is complex and admits of infinite variations."[6]

Sin concerns wrong behavior. You know the list—idolatry, murder, promiscuity, stealing, and lying. Yet we know sin goes deeper. It includes our thoughts and motives: hatred, envy, greed, malice, pride, and self-righteousness. Nursing anger against someone is like committing murder.

Sin is more than isolated actions or thoughts. All sin is deeply personal and relational. When we sin, we offend God, others, and self. Think about it—if we choose another god to worship besides God Almighty, we "cheat" on Him. Similarly, when we steal from someone, we undermine our bond with them.

Sin is serious. It wounds people and breaks relationships. The only way to restore these relationships is for Jesus to offer Himself to be wounded and broken on our behalf.

THE HIGH PRICE FOR OUR FORGIVENESS

After viewing Mel Gibson's *The Passion of the Christ*, many wondered why Jesus had to suffer so brutally. Hours of whipping, a wreath of thorns, spitting and mocking, hands being nailed to rough-sawn wood, all drawn out in painful, graphic detail.

Is this overkill?

The answer is "No!" Forgiveness is free, but it is not cheap. The highest price possible is paid that we might receive forgiveness as a free gift. The brutality of the cross is a measure of the horror of human sin. Put all hatred, malice, envy, lust, deceit, betrayal and all the wars, rapes, genocides, abuse, and oppression in humankind's sad history and you will understand the infinite price required and paid to remove our sin and provide forgiveness forever.

Yet, Jesus' death is not a tragedy. His suffering conquers sin and defeats death at the cross. It achieves reconciliation for you when you come to God for forgiveness of any crime, cruelty, or injustice. All you have to do is humbly ask.

When you confess your sins, you are completely washed clean of them. An anonymous saying captures this truth:

That Jesus died on the cross is history.
That Jesus died for sin is theology.
That Jesus died for my sin is Christianity.

As you read this, remember why Jesus died. Ask Him to apply His sacrifice to you and to forgive your sins. By His power and grace, become the renewed person He died for you to be.

THE CHALLENGE OF RECEIVING FORGIVENESS

The prick of our conscience often makes us aware of the seriousness of sin. But we need great assurances from God in order to find the humility and courage to confess our sins. We need the promises of God:

"Though your sins are like scarlet,
 they will be as white as snow;
though they are as red as crimson,
 they will become like wool." (Isa. 1:18)

If we confess our sins, he is faithful and just to forgive us our sins and to cleanse us from all unrighteousness. (1 John 1:9)

It takes grace to confess and grace to receive forgiveness. We can often struggle with residual guilt, rehearsing our faults again and again. What can we do about our reluctance to receive forgiveness? We must remember these great promises in Scripture, and we must remind ourselves that God forgets our sin once He forgives it.

FORGIVENESS IS AS COMPLETE AND FINISHED AS THE PERFECT SACRIFICE OF JESUS

This verse tells how Jesus is the only one who can remove the guilt and the power of sin:

> If anyone does sin, we have an advocate with the Father, Jesus Christ the righteous. He is the propitiation for our sins, and not for ours only but also for the sins of the whole world. (1 John 2:1-2)

The principle is this—don't dwell on your sin and guilt, but look steadily at Jesus. His sacrifice has infinite value to cancel your debt. Your sins are forever nailed to the cross.

THE CHALLENGE AND JOY OF LEARNING TO FORGIVE OTHERS

When we ask for forgiveness, it is received "as we also have forgiven our debtors." Receiving forgiveness is only half the picture. Jesus teaches that we must extend forgiveness to others as well, without exception: "For if you forgive other people when they sin against you, your heavenly Father will also forgive you. But if you do not forgive others their sins, your Father will not forgive your sins" (Matt. 6:14–15 NIV).

Let me elaborate on these weighty words. In order to be forgiven by our heavenly Father, we must also forgive those who have wronged us. To be clear, Jesus is telling us to forgive without excuse, no matter how often or how deep the offense. We see this in an additional example: "Then Peter came to Jesus and asked, 'Lord, how many times shall I forgive my brother or sister who sins against me? Up to seven times?' Jesus answered, 'I tell you, not seven times, but seventy-seven times'" (Matt. 18:21–22 NIV).

Overlooking a fault is possible in the "misdemeanors" of life. A rough word, minor neglect, or criticism—such wounds often heal in their own time. What are we to do, however, with the "felonies" of life? Consider victims of adultery and wrongful divorce. Or those who are defrauded in business and investments and lose everything. Who can heal their bitter disappointment? Forgiveness and reconciliation can seem like a distant and impossible dream.

Yet, forgiving those who sin against us is possible. It is also absolutely necessary. If you are the victim, you can never be fully healed without forgiveness. The torn relationship will continue to bring you pain. A bitter and unforgiving heart only hurts the victim.

> **Sin is a kind of toxic waste that lasts forever if not removed by forgiveness.**

Jesus understands the challenge and danger of not forgiving others. There are at least three very good reasons for Jesus' strong stand on forgiving others.

First, by reason of comparison. The debt owed to us cannot compare with the debt we owe to God. Nor can the small sacrifice I pay to forgive someone compare with the price Jesus paid.

The second reason is logic. When we ask for forgiveness, we need to confess all of our sins. Over years, Miroslav Volf struggled with hatred and a desire for revenge against the Serbian forces that ravaged his Croatian homeland. God taught him the important lesson about forgiving others: "We never forget that there is an evil worse than the original crime. It consists of self-centered slothfulness of the mind, heart, and will that will not recognize one's own sinfulness, not pursue justice for the innocent, and not extend grace to the guilty."[7]

A third reason we forgive others is that not forgiving can kill our own heart. As someone once said, "Unforgiveness is the poison

I drink trying to kill you." An unforgiving heart breeds grudges and bitterness—eventually killing the capacity to love. When we harbor an unforgiving heart, we rob ourselves of the release of forgiveness.

Sin is a kind of toxic waste that lasts forever if not removed by forgiveness. There was a company that tried to drill a mile-deep hole to bury toxic waste. A few years later, poisonous water surfaced. The buried PCBs contaminated the water, which seeped upwards through cracks and crevices in the underground rock.

This is how the sin of unforgiveness works. Hide it from yourself, and it will contaminate your heart. Bury it within, and a grudge will grow that seeps to the surface, poisoning the relationships in your world.

The only hope is concerted prayer as we ask for a spirit of contrition and confession—and wait for God to cleanse the soiled water of our souls.

GOD GIVES POWER AND HOPE TO FORGIVE OTHERS

For those wounded without an apology, there is hope. Jesus not only died to forgive us of our sins, but He gave His life to heal us of every wound we have had to suffer in a sinful and violent world:

> Surely he took up our pain
>> and bore our suffering,
> yet we considered him punished by God,
>> stricken by him, and afflicted.
> But he was pierced for our transgressions,
>> he was crushed for our iniquities;
> the punishment that brought us peace was upon him,
>> and by his wounds we are healed. (Isa. 53:4–5)

This healing makes it possible for us to forgive others—from the heart. Even while you are healing, you can also take your "enemy" to Jesus in prayer. Prayer is the first and most important step in restoring relations with others. As theologian Dietrich Bonhoeffer once said, "I can no longer condemn or hate a brother for whom I pray, no matter how much trouble he causes me."[8] The more we pray for our enemy, in time the Holy Spirit softens our hearts to release the hurt and hostility, replacing it with a genuine desire for God to forgive them of their offense.

After this, only when your heart is ready and it is safe to do so, Jesus encourages you to go to your offender and seek reconciliation. He tells us, "If your brother sins against you, go and tell him his fault, between you and him alone. If he listens to you, you have gained your brother" (Matt. 18:15).

This "intervention" requires wisdom and patience. We must ask for love and courage in order to be effective. We must also ask for God to open the door for the right opportunity. As He hears our prayers, the hope for reconciliation becomes real.

In my own life, it took years of prayer for me to gather the courage to speak to someone who had hurt me. Fear of rejection kept me from seeing the truth—or even acknowledging my hurt and their fault. I prayed about this. Then one day he and I got together, and God opened the door for meaningful conversation. It went wonderfully. In fact, after willingly acknowledging his fault, he also confronted me about my resentment and arrogance. We both felt better

> The more we pray for our enemy, in time the Holy Spirit softens our hearts to release the hurt and hostility, replacing it with a genuine desire for God to forgive them of their offense.

afterwards. We experienced reconciliation through forgiveness. Our relationship has been growing ever since.

FORGIVENESS RESULTS IN RELATIONAL RECONCILIATION

Reconciliation is the key to lasting and growing relationships with others. I think of my marriage. Caron and I have been together for over forty years and, through many bumps and bruises, our love has continually grown. The key is not compatibility or strength of character. The secret is reconciliation through forgiveness.

Saying "I am sorry" and "I forgive you" improves a marriage. Parent-child relationships also grow and deepen with an honest admission of failings—on both sides.

In the workplace and public arena we experience power politics, labor strife, and racial and class conflict. Without reconciliation, we will destroy one another. Jesus says, "Blessed are the peacemakers" (Matt. 5:9). A Christian peacemaker is someone who prays and works for reconciliation because he or she has been forgiven and reconciled to God.

God promises answers to our prayer: "Seek the peace and prosperity of the city to which I have carried you into exile. Pray to the LORD for it, because if it prospers, you too will prosper" (Jer. 29:7 NIV).

The practice of forgiveness can be applied to every relationship, no matter how deep the problem. Broken family relationships need healing. Marriages lie in scattered shards of unresolved

> A Christian peacemaker is someone who prays and works for reconciliation because he or she has been forgiven and reconciled to God.

114

hurt. Friends are separated by careless words. An office team loses friendship and chemistry. A church is reduced to gossip and accusation. Fill in your own blank. Nothing is beyond the reach of Jesus.

Prayerful Pondering

DAY   1   2   3   4   5   (6)   7

(1) Where do you struggle to receive forgiveness—either
something you feel unworthy of (a sin that feels too
difficult to forgive) or something you feel unapologetic
for (a sin that you don't see as a sin)?

(2) Where do you struggle with an unforgiving heart?
How has holding onto unforgiveness affected your life?
Are you able to bring it to Jesus as a first step?

(3) Which situational or relational conflicts in the immediate
world around you could use your prayers and
peacemaking actions?

Prayer Prompts

WHEN WE PRAY, "FORGIVE US OUR DEBTS, AS WE ALSO HAVE FORGIVEN OUR DEBTORS":

- We thank Jesus for the high price He paid to make forgiveness and reconciliation possible. We bring our hearts to Jesus for cleansing and our wounds to His healing streams.

- As we are forgiven, and as we receive healing, we find grace, courage, and power to forgive others who have sinned against us. We bring them to Jesus in prayer. We ask for God to open the door for the right opportunities for reconciliation.

- We pray to be peacemakers in the relationships and situations in the world around us.

My Personal Prayers

Borrow the prayers that express what is in your heart, or add your own.

TO FATHER GOD   **TODAY IS**   MM / DD / YY

PRAYER SPOT: Work   Home   School   _____

PATTERN FORGIVE US OUR DEBTS AS WE ALSO HAVE FORGIVEN OUR DEBTORS

PRIORITY RECEIVING FORGIVENESS & SEEKING RECONCILED RELATIONSHIPS

REQUEST EMPOWER US TO KNOW YOUR FORGIVENESS SO WE CAN FORGIVE OTHERS

MY LIFE

THANK YOU FOR BEING A FORGIVING GOD WHEN WE CONFESS OUR SIN. I ADMIT THAT MY REACTION TO CONFESSION AND SIN IS TO:

☐ AVOID IT, FEEL DEFENSIVE, AND FEEL LIKE I'VE DONE NOTHING WRONG

☐ FOCUS TOO MUCH ON IT OR FEEL GUILTY

☐

☐

GIVE ME HUMILITY AND COURAGE TO SEE WHERE I HAVE HURT YOU, MYSELF, OR OTHERS THROUGH MY ACTIONS, THOUGHTS, AND ATTITUDES:

☐

☐

My Personal Prayers

IS THERE ANYONE WHOM I NEED TO ASK FORGIVENESS FROM?

- [ ] WHO I HAVE HURT
- [ ] WHO I'VE HELD A GRUDGE AGAINST
- [ ]
- [ ]

I'M SORRY FOR WHAT I'VE DONE. FORGIVE ME OF MY SIN AND GUILT. AS I RECEIVE YOUR AMAZING GRACE AND FORGIVENESS, EMPOWER ME TO BE GRACIOUS TO FORGIVE OTHERS AS YOU FORGIVE ME. HELP ME TO FORGIVE:

- [ ]
- [ ]

GIVE ME THE HEART TO BE WILLING AND TAKE STEPS TO FORGIVE. HEAL ME FROM THE EFFECTS OF HOLDING ON TO UNFORGIVENESS:

- [ ]
- [ ]

My Personal Prayers

MY CITY

WHEN I LOOK AT MY CITY, I PRAY FOR THE AREAS AND ISSUES THAT NEED RECONCILIATION AND RESTORATION:

I PRAY FOR YOU TO PRESERVE THE PEACE OF THE CITY. EMPOWER US AS CITIZENS WITH YOUR LOVE & FORGIVENESS. HELP ME TO BE A PEACEMAKER IN MY INTERACTIONS & RELATIONSHIPS:

☐ FILL ME WITH PATIENCE, EMPATHY, PERSPECTIVE.

☐

MY GRATITUDE

THANK YOU, FATHER, FOR:

MY RESPONSE

NEW REVELATIONS, THOUGHTS, HEART CHANGES, OR STEPS I FEEL COMPELLED BY YOU TO TAKE:

. . . in Jesus' Name, Amen

DAY 1 2 3 4 5 6 **7**

Lead Us Not into Temptation but Deliver Us from Evil

"To have prayed well is to have fought well."
—Edward McKendree Bounds

*"The devil trembles when he sees
God's weakest child on his knees."*
—Anonymous

PILGRIM'S PROGRESS BY JOHN BUNYAN
IS ONE OF THE MOST POPULAR PARABLES
IN THE ENGLISH LANGUAGE. The main character,
Christian, is on a pilgrimage from the City of Destruction to the
Celestial City.

He faces seen and unseen foes. He falls into the Slough of
Despond, spends time in Doubting Castle, and is tempted by
sensual pleasure and ambition in the city Vanity Fair. In a crucial
battle, he goes head to head with Apollyon (another name for
Satan), who is the malevolent "ruler of this world." Christian
defends himself with the shield of faith and the sword of truth.
He is guarded by "All Prayer"—the comprehensive defense and
weapon of faith.

Bunyan's imagery is close to the biblical language and
metaphor. The Christian life is a war within a journey. We need
prayer for the battle. We need prayer for the journey—each
and every day. When we pray, "Lead us not into temptation,
but deliver us from evil," we are asking for at least four things.
First, we ask for God to lead us. Second, we pray for eyes of

faith. Third, we ask God to defend us from temptations and trials. Fourth, we ask for God's presence and power.

1. IN THIS JOURNEY, WE ASK FOR GOD TO LEAD US

When we pray "lead us not into temptation," we are implicitly asking our heavenly Father to be our guide and companion through the journey and battles of life until, safe at last, we come home to His heavenly kingdom.

God taught the lesson of His leading to the Israelites as they journeyed for forty years through the wilderness. He went before them in a pillar of cloud by day and a pillar of fire by night. The pillar is a picture of the Holy Spirit. Being led by that Spirit is a summary of the Christian journey: "For all who are led by the Spirit of God are sons of God" (Rom. 8:14).

When we pray "lead us not into temptation," we acknowledge that life's path is often hard and painful. Here, "temptation" is used in its original sense to mean the trial and testing of our faith. Of course, we can be tempted in our thoughts, motives, words, or deeds. But beneath every temptation, at a basic level, is the testing of our faith.

Consider the original temptation of Adam and Eve in the garden of Eden (Gen. 3). Yes, Satan makes the forbidden fruit look delicious and desirable for wisdom. Before this, however, the tempter insinuates doubt in God's word, *Did God actually say . . . ?* Eve goes for the bait and is trapped. We see that betraying trust in God happens first, eating the forbidden fruit follows. This is a common pattern: faith falters, then acts of disobedience ensue.

Consider Jesus' temptation for forty days in the wilderness. As the second Adam, Jesus reenacts the original temptation. But unlike Adam, in reply to each of Satan's temptations, Jesus affirms His faith in God and His word, answering simply, "It is written" (Luke 4:1-13).

When we ask God to lead us not into temptation, we are praying that He will give us grace to face, courage to endure, and power to overcome every lie of the enemy that would cause us to question God.

Jesus provides another perfect example of trusting His heavenly Father when He faces trial and testing in the garden of Gethsemane: "Going a little farther he fell on his face and prayed, saying, 'My Father, if it be possible, let this cup pass from me; nevertheless, not as I will, but as you will'" (Matt. 26:39). Jesus is asking, if possible, to be led away from the last trial—dying on a cross. At the same time, He is praying for grace to accept God's leading and for courage to endure it. We pray alongside Jesus when we ask, "Lead us not into temptation." Like Jesus, we experience suffering and loss. We endure the test. Following Him, we come through to victory.

> **When we ask God to lead us not into temptation, we are praying that He will give us grace to face, courage to endure, and power to overcome every lie of the enemy.**

2. IN ORDER TO PERSEVERE, WE NEED EYES OF FAITH TO SEE THE WHOLE PICTURE

Albert Einstein was perhaps the greatest genius of the twentieth century. When he devised the theories of special and general relativity, it was assumed that he discovered the key to understanding the universe. However, as late as 1924, Einstein and everyone else thought that the Milky Way constituted the universe. Now we know that there are as many as one hundred billion other galaxies in the universe—each with more than one hundred billion stars! Einstein "saw" only a small part of the picture.

In much the same way, the world before our eyes is only a small part of life. We should invite new discovery, welcome new paradigms, and not hold tightly to a safe and familiar picture. We can continue to explore and enjoy the universe we see but must be open to a far greater reality of which this seen world is only a part.

Where does prayer fit in this? Prayer is like the Hubble telescope, orbiting 340 miles above the earth's surface, lifting us far above the earth's perspective to see the entire cosmos. As we pray, we begin to see the universe as God sees it, glimpses of invisible galaxies come into view.

This directly relates to our request, "Lead us not into temptation." Because God creates everything visible and invisible, these two "halves" of existence (the earthly and the heavenly) are deeply related and in constant interplay. Forces of good and evil are in constant conflict.

This is the Christian worldview. Every person, community, church, and Christian is engaged in a very real battle against temptation, guilt, and despair. The instrument of attack can be other people, social forces, media, unseen personalities, or simply one's own unbelief and self-doubt.

This fight matters. If we quit and give in, there will be no victory. Yet ultimately, in the final hour, Jesus Himself will physically appear with His angels and defeat all of His and our enemies.

> Be alert and of sober mind. Your enemy the devil prowls around like a roaring lion looking for someone to devour. Resist him, standing firm in the faith, because you know that the family of believers throughout the world is undergoing the same kind of sufferings.
>
> And the God of all grace, who called you to his eternal

glory in Christ, after you have suffered a little while, will himself restore you and make you strong, firm and steadfast. To him be the power for ever and ever. (1 Peter 5:8–11 NIV)

Prayer connects us to the power and presence of Jesus, our coming King. As we pray in expectation, His resurrection life flows into our hearts by the Holy Spirit He gives us. He enables us to defend against every seen and unseen enemy and to advance in His promised victory.

3. WE ASK GOD TO DEFEND US FROM TEMPTATIONS AND TRIALS

In this visible/invisible battle we fight different varieties of temptation on different fronts. There are at least four battle lines where temptation occurs.

First, we are tempted through the weakness of our fallen nature. Inordinate desire, deviant passion, envy and avarice, arrogance, hatred, and pride are within each of us. As Dorothy Sayers calls it, this "interior dislocation of the soul"[9] accounts for much of the bloodshed, brokenness, and betrayal found in the human story. Our own inner compulsion (not God or the devil) leads us into every temptation:

> When tempted, no one should say, "God is tempting me." For God cannot be tempted by evil, nor does he tempt anyone; but each person is tempted when they are dragged away by their own evil desire and enticed. Then, after desire has conceived, it gives birth to sin; and sin, when it is full-grown, gives birth to death. (James 1:13–15 NIV)

Second, temptation surrounds us. As pollution clogs the air of the cities of the world, so we live in an atmosphere of temptation. We need prayer to breathe the fresh air of heaven. And we need it in special measure in a world where media has made the lure of temptation far more potent. For example, sexual exploitation and predation are fueled by promiscuous sitcoms, salacious talk shows, and seductive advertising. Through the internet, base passions are excited with increasing frequency and intensity.

Little is being done to slow the avalanche. Moral outrage is reserved for those who would try to restrict access to this "information." One person noted, "Even to avoid evil makes one a marked man." We pray fervently to withstand temptation because we are constantly surrounded by it.

Third, moral and spiritual assault comes in the form of false teaching. Take the popular adventure novel *The Da Vinci Code* by Dan Brown, which represents Jesus as a pagan leader who participated in ritual sex and sired children through Mary Magdalene. Though none of the alleged documents the author uses to support his argument have ever been discovered, these lies are represented to the reader as history.

Because so few know the Bible's portrait of Jesus, enormous numbers are drawn in and are dead serious about Brown's viewpoints—even though they are the basis of a fictional story![10] The Bible warns that, in every age, new false "Christs" will arise. The objective of these "antichrists" is to mislead believers and to prevent others from getting to know who Jesus really is. Jesus warned, "Watch out that no one deceives you. For many will come in my name, claiming, 'I am the Messiah,' and will deceive many" (Matt. 24:4–5 NIV).

When we pray, "Lead us not into temptation," we pray for faith to resist false teachings about Christ.

Fourth, back to our original assertion, the trials, sufferings, and betrayals of life tempt us to question or even abandon our faith in God. It is really this doubting of God that is at the root of every temptation.

Our spiritual life is like a ship. Faith is the hull. In naval warfare, if the hull is strong and holds, little significant damage results from a cannon attack. Only if cannon balls pierce the hull is there penetration to the heart of the vessel.

In the same way, every assault of evil is first directed at this hull—our faith. Using accusation, trial, and temptation, Satan wants to wreck our connection to God and for us to question His goodness, power, and love. If he succeeds, the hull is breached and we begin to sink. Once we doubt the goodness, grace, and power of God, we are immediately vulnerable.

On our own we are outgunned and outmanned by a superior enemy. But as we pray, Jesus strengthens and comforts us when we are tempted. The apostle Paul encourages us: "No temptation has overtaken you that is not common to man. God is faithful, and he will not let you be tempted beyond your ability, but with the temptation he will also provide the way of escape, that you may be able to endure it" (1 Cor. 10:13).

Paul is not saying that we will never fall into sin. What he means is that, though we will be tempted and sometimes fail, by His grace and power we will grow in faith and live to fight another day.

As we ask God not to lead us into temptation, our greatest encouragement is Jesus Himself. He endured every temptation Satan could throw at Him (Luke 4:1–13). One reason He did all this is so that He would be able to defend and protect us against every temptation we face: "Because he himself suffered when he was tempted, he is able to help those who are being tempted" (Heb. 2:18 NIV).

4. EXPERIENCING GOD'S PRESENCE AND POWER: HOW GOD'S KINGDOM ADVANCES

This prayer moves from defense, "Lead us not into temptation," to offense, "Deliver us from evil." Ultimately, we not only survive the battles of life, we win. The reason for this is Jesus. His victory over sin and death at the cross and empty tomb is decisive and complete. The present age is a brief moment of history and the final "wrap-up" is soon coming. It is like the end of World War II. The decisive battle for the Allied victory is fought and won at Normandy. After this battle, it is only one year until complete surrender and the signing of treaties.

In prayer, by faith, a believer appropriates and participates in Jesus' victory in every spiritual and practical area of this life. The victory we share with Jesus is seen and unseen, practical and spiritual.

> **Prayer is the key to victory in all spiritual warfare.**

For example, for a number of years our church worked with a local ministry called Genesis Vancouver (now called SA Foundation), which helps sexually exploited women and their children. When we pray for one of these women to be delivered from evil, we desire her to experience the grace of forgiveness and spiritual healing. We also ask for her to be delivered from the pimps, "Johns," and abusive people who prey on her and use her as a slave. Anything less would be less than Jesus intends. N.T. Wright said,

> This is part of the prayer for the Kingdom: it is the prayer that the forces of destruction, of dehumanization, of anti-creation, of anti-redemption may be bound and gagged, and that God's good world may escape from being sucked down into their morass.[11]

As John Wesley once said, "There is no Christianity that is not a social Christianity." When we pray, "Deliver us from evil," we include social justice and mercy: "He has told you, O man, what is good; and what does the LORD require of you but to do justice, and to love kindness, and to walk humbly with your God?" (Mic. 6:8).

Prayer is the key to victory in all spiritual warfare. Theologian Karl Barth once said, "To clasp the hands in prayer is the beginning of an uprising against the disorder of the world." When we pray, God will give us courage for each day's battle—and He also promises to act: "For he delivers the needy when he calls, the poor and him who has no helper. He has pity on the weak and the needy, and saves the lives of the needy. From oppression and violence he redeems their life, and precious is their blood in his sight" (Ps. 72:12–14).

Prayerful Pondering

1 What battles are you personally fighting?

2 How can prayer give you courage and hope?

3 Where in the world around you do you see conflict between light and dark forces? What injustices can you pray for?

Prayer Prompts

WHEN WE PRAY, "LEAD US NOT INTO TEMPTATION, BUT DELIVER US FROM EVIL":

- We ask to recognize God's guidance and presence with us, receive Jesus' resurrection power to resist temptation, and endure and overcome trials.

- We pray for others who are entangled in difficulties or trials and pray for Jesus to defend and deliver them.

- We pray for the restraint of evil forces in our city and world. We pray for God's goodness and power to prevail.

My Personal Prayers

DAY   1   2   3   4   5   6   7

Borrow the prayers that express what is in your heart, or add your own.

TO FATHER GOD   **TODAY IS**   MM / DD / YY

PRAYER SPOT: Work   Home   School   _____

PATTERN   LEAD US NOT INTO TEMPTATION BUT DELIVER US FROM EVIL
PRIORITY   FOLLOWING AND TRUSTING YOUR LEADERSHIP
REQUEST   GUIDE AND RESCUE IN JESUS' VICTORY

MY LIFE

THANK YOU THAT YOU WANT TO LEAD ME THROUGH THE JOURNEY OF
LIFE. I PRAY YOU WOULD GUIDE ME THROUGH MY PRESENT CHALLENGES:

- ☐
- ☐

IN MY STRUGGLES I FEEL:

- ☐ WEAK
- ☐ HOPEFUL
- ☐
- ☐

- ☐ OVERWHELMED
- ☐ WILLING TO FIGHT

- ☐ STUCK
- ☐ INDIFFERENT

My Personal Prayers

SHOW ME WHERE YOU ARE PRESENT AND GUIDING ME:

☐ FILL ME WITH YOUR POWER AND COURAGE TO ENDURE.

☐ GIVE ME WISDOM TO LEAD ME FORWARD.

☐

☐

MY CITY

I PRAY FOR THOSE WHO DAILY BATTLE AND THE FORCES THAT LEAD TO:

☐ SUFFERING   ☐ ADDICTIONS   ☐ OPPRESSION

☐ ABUSE   ☐ MENTAL ILLNESS   ☐ EXPLOITATION

☐

☐

RESCUE THOSE WHO ARE STRUGGLING; BRING THEM NEAR TO YOU
TO KNOW YOUR COMPASSION, PRESENCE, AND POWER IN THEIR
CHALLENGES.

DAY 1   2   3   4   5   6   (7)

LET YOUR LIGHT SHINE STRONGER THAN THE DARKNESS. SHOW ME THE
PRACTICAL WAYS I CAN BE INVOLVED IN FIGHTING THE GOOD FIGHT.

☐

☐

GIVE ME COURAGE AND WISDOM TO MEANINGFULLY BE INVOLVED.

MY GRATITUDE

THANK YOU, FATHER, FOR:

MY RESPONSE

NEW REVELATIONS, THOUGHTS, HEART CHANGES, OR STEPS I FEEL
COMPELLED BY YOU TO TAKE:

. . . in Jesus' Name, Amen

THE REST OF YOUR LIFE

Amen

*"To be a Christian without prayer
is no more possible than
to be alive without breathing."*
—Frank Laubach

OUR FATHER IN HEAVEN,
HALLOWED BE YOUR NAME.
YOUR KINGDOM COME,
YOUR WILL BE DONE,
  ON EARTH AS IT IS IN HEAVEN.
GIVE US THIS DAY OUR DAILY BREAD,
AND FORGIVE US OUR DEBTS,
  AS WE ALSO HAVE FORGIVEN OUR
    DEBTORS.
AND LEAD US NOT INTO TEMPTATION,
  BUT DELIVER US FROM EVIL.

(Matt. 6:9–13)

This is the prayer of Jesus, God's only Son. God the Father always hears His Son. And because we are united to Christ, He will also always hear the prayers of each of us, His adopted sons and daughters. By giving us this prayer, Jesus calls us to pray it faithfully, invites us to pray it personally, and desires us to pray it as a community.

We find a dramatic illustration of the power of this call to pray in *The Lord of the Rings* trilogy. In this Tolkien tale—and the movie series based on it—the citizens of Middle Earth have created a system of beacons, or signal fires. They are massive piles of dry timber, stacked in readiness on highly visible mountaintops. A lit torch is always ready for a pair of sentries to light the beacon the instant they are called.

This signal fire kindles the memory of ancient allegiances—a united people against a common enemy. When under attack, the ancient city of Gondor will light its beacons, and all of Middle Earth will gather to defend her. It is a summons and signal for the return of the king.

As the story the *Return of the King* unfolds, the great city of Gondor finds itself in trouble. Completely outnumbered, it is surrounded by legions of enemies. Huge catapults hurl monstrous rocks to break its walls. A massive cast-iron battering ram tears through its gates. Behind this army is the hideous strength of Sauron—the evil spirit. His consuming purpose is to destroy the race of men and to prevent the return of the king.

Within the city is another enemy. Denethor, the steward of Gondor, is assigned to protect the city and prepare it for the coming king. But in the movie, when the threat of destruction

> By giving us the Lord's Prayer, Jesus calls us to pray it faithfully, invites us to pray it personally, and desires us to pray it as a community.

is imminent, he refuses to do his part. He has studied the might and power of his enemy, and his heart is filled with despair. "All hope is lost," he says. Worst of all, he refuses to light the beacons and summon Middle Earth to war.

We see parallels in our present situation. We might value and enjoy our modern world, but our cities and our churches have enemies—within and without.

Relativism and hedonism break down the concept of truth and eat away at the foundations of right and wrong. There is no end of opponents attacking the simple truths of the gospel. New Age, a return to the spirits of paganism, is growing. Television, radio, magazines, and the internet bury us in advertising, shape us into voracious consumers, and divert us from higher purposes. Relationships are reduced to sexual encounters.

This avalanche seems unstoppable. Ethical and religious concerns are dismissed and ridiculed. Many have resigned the field in frustration or despair. Some have joined the other side.

Behind this assault is an insidious, malevolent force. He is intent on crushing and eliminating any sense of eternal or transcendent purpose. In the meantime, within the city and within the church, like Denethor, the children of the King are strangely inactive. A foreboding calm settles over church and city. There is fear in the air. Our enemy smells it.

Yet there is a faithful remnant who knows what needs to be done. Jesus is calling us to light the beacons of prayer. When we pray Jesus' prayer, we make a great discovery. We recover our identity as children of the King. At its heart, this prayer is a yearning for the return of the King to rescue and deliver all those who wait for Him.

THE DIFFERENCE PRAYER MAKES

In the battle for Middle Earth, the tide turns when Gondor's beacon is lit. Seeing its flames, one beacon after another explodes in fire. The land is lit with hope. The long-awaited king, Aragorn, sees the flaming beacons and prepares his return. It is time for him to assert his rightful rule and reign over Middle Earth. It is time to rescue the innocent. It is time to vanquish the enemy.

A similar scenario occurs when God's people set themselves to pray. To pray is to light the beacons. To pray Jesus' prayer is to summon the people of God to a united warfare of love and truth. It is a mighty cry for our King to lead us in battle.

Like flaming beacons, the fire of prayer is contagious. As this prayer begins to burn, the hearts of others will burn too. We unite to defend each other and to defend our neighbor and our cities. Hope replaces despair. Readiness to act replaces apathy. We experience the might of grace to overcome hatred and violence.

The present and coming King Himself will visit us.

At the critical moment, Aragorn the rightful king, returns to the city. The armies of Sauron have no defense against such an opponent. In a matter of minutes the city is regained, the besieged are rescued, and every foe is leveled to the ground. Jesus is the present and coming King.

When He comes, no enemy can withstand Him. He storms the gates of the city in answer to prayer. He renews His church, transforms communities, rebuilds cities, and makes our streets safe to dwell in.

> To pray Jesus' prayer is to summon the people of God to a united warfare of love and truth. It is a mighty cry for our King to lead us in battle.

The seven purposes of Jesus will come to light as we pray His prayer. He gives us hearts that cry out, "Abba, Father!" His kingdom will come. Men, women, and children will be saved. His will shall be done in the streets of the city—with wisdom, love, and courage. Simplicity and generosity will characterize us, His children. We will enjoy daily bread with thanksgiving. Bitter feuds will be resolved as we learn to receive and extend forgiveness. We will move from defending against temptations to advancing in spiritual battles.

He will hear and answer as we pray:

> "If my people, who are called by my name, will humble themselves and pray and seek my face and turn from their wicked ways, then I will hear from heaven, and I will forgive their sin and will heal their land." (2 Chron. 7:14 NIV)

Come, Jesus. Come!

WHAT IT MEANS WHEN YOU SAY "AMEN."

"Amen" is a confident expression of the heart, meaning, "It will surely be as God has promised!" To end our prayer on this high note assumes our prayer has been full of faith that God will hear and give us what we ask for. Praying with this kind of assurance is exactly why Jesus taught us the Lord's Prayer.

For example, since we know our Father will hear us, we want to be sure we are asking Him for the right things. Otherwise, a cloud of doubt hovers over our prayer. To remove the cloud and have our prayers filled with light, Jesus gave us several specific requests. With these as a sure guide, we can be confident that we are asking for what pleases Him.

We also know that our thoughts often wander as we pray, and our feelings get all muddled and confused. As we learn to pray the way Jesus taught us, and with the help of His indwelling Spirit, our motives and intent grow in steadiness, so now we can approach God with sincere feelings, filled with hope.

When we ask what is pleasing to the Father, and we pray with a sincere heart, we can finish each prayer with a hearty "Amen!"

When we say "Amen" aloud and with feeling, it is an announcement to one another and a pledge to God. Think of the rousing cheer of a gathering sports team after a hard-fought victory. Encircling and clasping their hands together, their rejoicing cry encourages each other and rises up to the surrounding crowds. Their cheer means, "Victory is achieved!" After our hard work in prayer, we can clasp our hands together and announce "Amen!" Just by saying the word with confidence, we lift up one another in bright hope. At the same time, we affirm to our Father in heaven that we believe He will give us all He has told us to ask for.

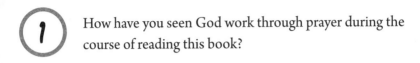

THE REST OF YOUR LIFE

1 How have you seen God work through prayer during the course of reading this book?

2 How will you light your beacon?

3 Imagine: How would your life look if you began to consistently pray through the priorities of the Lord's Prayer? What are one or two ways you can integrate the Lord's Prayer into your life?

Prayer Practice

THE REST OF YOUR LIFE

After your prayers, try saying "Amen!" confidently and out loud.

My Personal Prayers

THE REST OF YOUR LIFE

Borrow the prayers that express what is in your heart, or add your own.

TO FATHER GOD   **TODAY IS** MM / DD / YY

PRAYER SPOT: Work   Home   School   _____

MY PRAYER

THANK YOU FOR THE GOOD WORK YOU'VE STARTED IN MY LIFE THROUGH PRAYER. CONTINUE THE GOOD WORK: KEEP TEACHING ME HOW TO PRAY.

MY GRATITUDE

THANK YOU, GOD, FOR:

MY RESPONSE

NEW REVELATIONS, THOUGHTS, HEART CHANGES, OR STEPS I FEEL COMPELLED TO TAKE:

. . . in Jesus' Name, Amen

Appendix

A Prayer Grid to Build the Coming Kingdom

Here is a simple sequence to help you focus on one portion of the Lord's Prayer at a time by praying through each priority in the grid (i.e. one row) from left to right. Take for example praying through the first pattern and priority: God as Father.

1. UPWARD (PATTERN & PRIORITY)

- Start your prayer by focusing on the priority upward to God, beginning by acknowledging God as Father.

- Praise Jesus for the priority, for adoption as sons and daughters into God's family.

- Meditate on the priority of being a child of God. Ask the Holy Spirit to show you what it means. What does the priority, this reality, tell you about God?

2. INWARD (PASSIONS)

- Next pray the priority, the truth of your identity, **into your heart.** Talk with God about it.

- How is the priority **growing or lacking** in your heart and life?

3. OUTWARD (PEOPLE)

- **What will your life look like** as this priority takes deeper root, as you acknowledge and know God to be Father? Ask Jesus to **transform your heart** and life to be more like His.

- Now pray for **others to experience more of God's promises** and priority in their lives and that they would come to know Him as Father.

- Pray for **the world, the church, and the city,** especially as needs relate to the priority at hand.

4. UPWARD (PRAISE)

- End by **praising God** for His blessings and answers to prayer. **Recognize** how God has been present. **Thank** Him.

For further elaboration on using this prayer sequence/grid, please see *Seven Days of Prayer with Jesus* by John Smed from www.prayercurrent.com/

PATTERN	Our **Father** in heaven	**Hallowed** be your name	Your **kingdom** come	**Your will** be done, on earth as it is in heaven	Give us this day our **daily bread**	**Forgive us** our debts, as we also have forgiven our debtors	**Lead us** not into temptation, but deliver us from evil
PRIORITY & PROMISE	Relationship Prayer	Worship	Evangelism City renewal	Mercy Social justice	Contentment Generosity Simplicity	Unity Reconciliation	Guidance Advance
Pray God's **PASSIONS** into my own heart							
Pray God's blessing for other **PEOPLE**							
PRAISE for who He is & thank Him for answers to prayers							

Acknowledgments

I am deeply grateful to Nathan Vanderclippe for initiating a fresh "pocket book" approach to *Journey in Prayer*. A special thanks to Duane Sherman at Moody Publishers, whose passion for prayer opened doors for this book. I am also grateful to Mackenzie Conway, who added fresh insights and enthusiasm to what could have been an otherwise tedious editing process.

Notes

1. Annie Dillard, *Teaching A Stone to Talk: Expeditions and Encounters* (New York: Harper Perennial, 2013), 94.

2. Martin Luther, *A Simple Way to Pray: Martin Luther, the 16th Century Reformer, Tells His Barber How to Empower His Prayer Life* (Serve International, Inc, 2003).

3. I speak of urban renewal and use the word "city" because city is often the word used in the Bible when referring to a group of people who choose to live in proximity to one another under common laws and government—this includes rural communities, suburbs, metropolitans, and the like. Each "city" has a unique collective personality and history, and we are to pray for our city's renewal.

4. Robert Burns, "Selkirk Grace."

5. Martin Turcotte, "Charitable Giving by Individuals," Spotlight on Canadians: Results from the General Social Survey, Statistics Canada, December 16, 2015, https://www150.statcan.gc.ca/n1/pub/89-652-x/89-652-x2015008-eng.htm.

6. Quoted in *Not the Way It's Supposed to Be* by Cornelius Plantinga Jr. (Grand Rapids: Wm. B. Eerdmans, 1996), 39.

7. Miroslav Volf, "Original Crime, Primal Care," *God and the Victim*, Lisa Barnes Lampman. ed. (Grand Rapid, MI: Wm. B. Eerdmans, 1999), 35.

8. Dietrich Bonhoeffer, *Life Together: A Discussion of Christian Fellowship* (New York: Harper & Row, 1954).

9. Dorthy Sayers, *Creed or Chaos* (Manchester: Sophia Institute Press, 1995).

10. A good antidote to *The Da Vinci Code* is the book *Cracking Da Vinci's Code: You've Read the Fiction, Now Read the Facts* (Colorado Springs: David C. Cook, 2004) by James Garlow and Peter Jones.

11. N. T. Wright, *The Lord and His Prayer* (Grand Rapids: Wm. B. Eerdmans Publishing, 1997), 55.

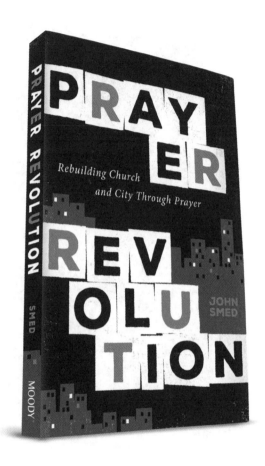

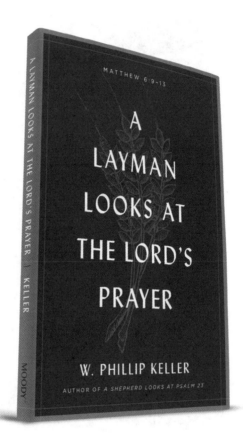

Collected insights from A.W. Tozer on common topics for the Christian life

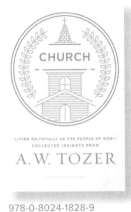

LIVING FAITHFULLY AS THE PEOPLE OF GOD—
COLLECTED INSIGHTS FROM

A.W. TOZER

978-0-8024-1828-9

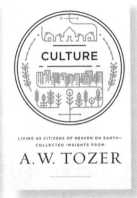

LIVING AS CITIZENS OF HEAVEN ON EARTH—
COLLECTED INSIGHTS FROM

A.W. TOZER

978-1-60066-801-2

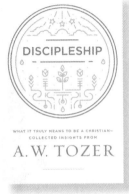

WHAT IT TRULY MEANS TO BE A CHRISTIAN—
COLLECTED INSIGHTS FROM

A.W. TOZER

978-1-60066-804-3

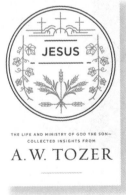

THE LIFE AND MINISTRY OF GOD THE SON—
COLLECTED INSIGHTS FROM

A.W. TOZER

978-0-8024-1520-2

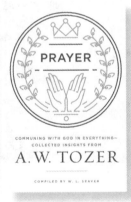

COMMUNING WITH GOD IN EVERYTHING—
COLLECTED INSIGHTS FROM

A.W. TOZER

COMPILED BY W. L. SEAVER

978-0-8024-1381-9

THE REASON WE WERE CREATED—
COLLECTED INSIGHTS FROM

A.W. TOZER

978-0-8024-1603-2

also available as eBooks

MOODY
Publishers®

From the Word to Life®

"The intelligent child of God must be driven to say, 'I must pray, pray, pray. I must put all my energy and all my heart into prayer. Whatever else I do, I must pray.'"

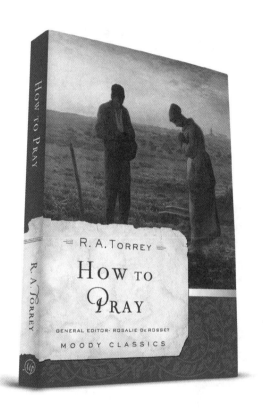

MOODY Publishers®

*From the Word **to** Life®*

Torrey examines praying in the Spirit, obstacles to prayer, the best times to pray, and more. Torrey outlines a practical strategy for living life in conversation with God.

978-0-8024-5652-6 | also available as an eBook